"*The Best Question Ever* delivers an indispensable principle for anyone wanting God's best. I heard Andy teach this material years ago and have been asking this question ever since."

"*The Best Question Ever* has become a permanent filter for all my decisions."

"I have seen this question totally transform the way students and adults approach decision making. It really is *The Best Question Ever*."

THE BEST QUESTION EVER

THE
BEST
QUESTION
EVER

?

ANDY STANLEY

Multnomah Books

THE BEST QUESTION EVER
published by Multnomah Books
A division of Random House, Inc.
© 2004 by Andy Stanley

International Standard Book Number: 978-1-59052-390-6

Interior design and typeset by Katherine Lloyd, The DESK

Unless otherwise indicated, Scripture quotations are from:
New American Standard Bible® © 1960, 1977, 1995
by the Lockman Foundation. Used by permission.

Other Scripture quotations are from:
The Holy Bible, *English Standard Version* (ESV) © 2001
by Crossway Bibles, a division of Good News Publishers.
Used by permission. All rights reserved.

The Holy Bible, New International Version (NIV)
© 1973, 1984 by International Bible Society,
used by permission of Zondervan Publishing House

Multnomah and its mountain colophon are registered trademarks
of Random House Inc.
Printed in the United States of America

For information:
MULTNOMAH BOOKS
12265 ORACLE BOULEVARD, SUITE 200
COLORADO SPRINGS, CO 80921

08 09 10—10 9 8 7 6

This book is dedicated to
Lanny Donoho.

_____

Solomon was right—there is a friend
who sticks closer than a brother. You have been
that kind of friend to me. Thank you.

Contents

Introduction

IF ONLY…

he Best Question Ever? Who do I think I am? We've never even met and I have written an entire book based on the premise that I know *the* question that trumps every other question you could ask about your life. And doesn't the word *Ever* hint of naïveté on my part? *Ever?* As in the history of mankind?

Perhaps I should have gone with *The Best Question I Know.* Or maybe, *A Really Good Question.* But the truth is, I believe the question I'm about to pose really *is* the Best Question Ever. For everybody.

This may not be the most *important* question ever; there are probably more important questions. But as you are about to discover, the Best Question Ever will help bring clarity to the important questions. A more important question for you might be, "Should I take this job?" Or, "Is she the one for me?" Or, "Does God want me to move?" "Lease or buy?" "Should I stay or leave?" The Best Question Ever will bring you fresh insight to all of these questions.

So what makes this question *the* best question? Three things. First, it can be applied to every decision you ever make for the rest of your life. Second, it is a question that is easy to answer; in most cases you will know the answer immediately. Third, it is a question that pierces the fog of self-deception.

Bottom line, what makes the Best Question Ever the best question ever is that it is the most *helpful* question ever.

LOOKING BACK

If the title of this book seems a bit over the top, my next statement may send you scrambling back to your local bookstore in search of a refund. In fact, I have been staring at my computer screen for the past fifteen minutes, wondering just how foolish it would be for me to make the claim I am about to make this early in the book. But having just read through the entire manuscript, I'm more convinced than ever.

So here goes.

Your greatest regret could have been avoided had you asked the Best Question Ever and then acted on your conclusion.

A bit strong?

Regardless of whether it is an action or event you regret or an entire chapter of your life that you wish you could do over, had you evaluated your options through the lens of this single powerful question, you would have avoided what may be your greatest ongoing source of pain. As you move through the pages that follow, you may find that this one question could have changed the trajectory of your entire life.

The Best Question Ever is a question I ask more than once every day. It is a question that guided me through my late twenties as a single man. It is a question that has served me well through sixteen incredible years of marriage. It is a question I have taught my three kids to ask about every option that comes their way. They know it is the lens through which we evaluate every decision we make as a family.

Over the past twenty years I have had the opportunity to teach this principle to thousands of middle-school and high school students. Many of them are adults now with children of their own. Letters, e-mails, and conversations assure me that the Best Question Ever continues to serve as a decision-making filter for scores of these young adults.

When I share the Best Question Ever with adult audiences, the response is nearly always the same: "I wish I had heard this years ago." Translated: "I could have avoided some regret if only…"

The Best Question Ever serves as a lens through which you can evaluate your options. It is a filter that casts things in their actual light. It is a grid that provides context for every decision. The Best Question Ever will provide you with a new perspective on your love life, your career, your finances, your family, your schedule—everything. The Best Question Ever will shed light on issues the Bible doesn't specifically address.

But the Best Question Ever is not always an easy question to ask. It can be a bit threatening. It exposes so much about our hearts and our motives that it is, well, it's just not an easy question to ask. That's just one more reason why it is the Best Question Ever.

LOOKING AHEAD

This book is divided into six sections. In section 1 you will be introduced to the Question. It takes me a couple of chapters to get to it, so be patient. In the three sections that follow, we will apply the Best Question Ever to three key areas of life: your time, your money, and your relationships. In section 5 I'm going to let you in on a secret known by all the world's best decision-makers. In the final section I'm going to challenge you to make a decision that will allow you to get the maximum benefit from the Best Question Ever.

The principle behind *The Best Question Ever* has impacted my decisions, and consequently my life, more than any other. This is more than another book for me. This is a life message. The content is not simply pulled from a series of sermons; it is drawn from the past twenty-two years of my life's journey.

All right, it is time to get started. I hope you enjoy the book. More importantly, I hope this powerful question becomes a permanent part of your decision-making process. If you have the courage to ask it, your Heavenly Father will use this simple question to guide and protect you in the days to come. And as you experience the difference this question makes, I think you will agree that it really is the Best Question Ever.

—Andy Stanley

Part I

THE QUESTION

1

DUMB AND DUMBER

Finding Common Ground

You and I have something in common. We've both done some really dumb stuff. Stuff we hope nobody ever finds out about. Stuff we wish we could forget. There's money we wish we hadn't spent, cars we wish we had never bought, investments we wish we hadn't made, invitations we wish we hadn't accepted, relationships we wish we had stayed out of, jobs we wish we had never taken, partnerships we never should have entered into, phone calls we never should have returned, contracts we never should have signed.

If you are like me, you look back and wonder, *How could I have been so dumb? So blind? So foolish?* We should have known better. In some cases, we did know better, but for some reason we thought we could beat the odds—that we would be the exceptions to the rule. In spite of what common sense (and maybe a friend or two) told us, we believed that we could control the outcome of our decisions.

So we followed our hearts, we trusted our emotions, we did our own thing, and now we wonder what in the world we were thinking.

If you're like most people, some of the decisions you wish you could unmake led to chapters of your life you wish you could go back and unlive. Picking a stock based on a bad tip is one thing; choosing a marriage partner without doing some due diligence is something else entirely. Making four $24.95 payments on something that's only worth $24.95 to begin with is embarrassing; $25,000 in credit card debt can ruin you.

Some of our bad decisions simply embarrass us. Others scar us.

What's obvious now wasn't so obvious then. And what's obvious to us now may not be so obvious to everybody around us. Chances are, you've already bumped into somebody on the verge of making the same dumb decision you made when you were his age. And, as I was, you were sure that once he heard your sad story, he would drop to his knees in gratitude for your life-changing insight. Having come to grips with the error of his ways, he would immediately reverse course, call off the marriage, pay cash, tear up the contract, dissolve the partnership, sell his drums, stay in school, or whatever.

But no. Instead, he endures our tales of woe, thanks us for the unsolicited advice, and continues full speed ahead into the oncoming train. And we think back and wonder,

*Could I have possibly been that naive? That stubborn? That
foolish?*

Yep.

POOR PLANNING

When we watch people we know—or strangers for that
matter—make foolish decisions, it's as if they are strategically and intentionally setting out to mess up their lives.

After all, it takes a lot of planning to marry the wrong
person. Any marriage, even a bad one, is not a casual
endeavor. Think of the time and energy it takes to set up a
doomed business partnership or to start a business that has
no hope of success. Think about all the paperwork people
have to wade through to purchase houses they can't really
afford or lease cars they are going to lose or apply for loans
they can't repay.

Having watched dozens of people methodically waste
their lives, potential, and money, I've concluded that while
nobody *plans* to mess up his life, the problem is that few of
us *plan not to*. That is, we don't put the necessary safeguards
in place to ensure a happy ending.

Nobody plans to destroy his marriage, but few people
take precautions that guarantee "as long as we both shall live."

Nobody plans to raise irresponsible, codependent children, but it's clear from looking at society that a bunch of
parents don't plan not to.

Nobody plans an addiction, but it happens. Why? A lack of necessary precaution.

I haven't talked to anyone who planned to be buried under a mountain of credit-card debt, but I've met a lot of people who didn't plan not to be.

Our poor planning leads precisely where we had no intention of going. And once there we ask, "How did this happen to me?"

The Best Question Ever will provide the answer.

Better yet, the Best Question Ever will help you stay out of the situations and circumstances that rob you of your potential, your opportunities, and your future.

2

A MOST UNCOMFORTABLE QUESTION

And the Courage to Ask It

At the age of twenty-five I came across three verses in Scripture that totally changed the way I made decisions. I suddenly had a new filter through which to evaluate every opportunity, invitation, and relationship—everything I was asked to do, everything I was tempted to become a part of. I began to consider my whole life through this new grid, a grid that boiled down to asking one simple question.

The reason I consider it the best question ever is that it has the potential to *foolproof* every aspect of your life. It will give you a new perspective on your love life, your career, your finances, your family, your schedule, everything. The

Best Question Ever sheds light on issues the Bible doesn't specifically address. The Best Question Ever provides you with a context for addressing questions of where to draw the line morally, relationally, and ethically. Like a piercing light, this powerful question cuts through the fog surrounding so many of your decisions and enables you to see clearly.

And yet, as you are about to discover, it's not an easy question to ask. It's not that the words are difficult to say. It's just that the question exposes so much about your heart and your motives that it is, well, it's just not an easy question to ask. It's like walking out of a dark building on a sunny day—there is something about this question that will make you want to retreat to the shadows where your eyes have already adjusted. Like direct sunlight to the unshielded eye, this question can be extremely uncomfortable.

Here's why.

THE ART OF SELF-DECEPTION

You see, in addition to making the occasional dumb decision, you and I have something else in common: We are good at deceiving ourselves. Really good.

Self-deception comes naturally to me. I can make a bad decision look and sound like a great decision with one hand tied behind my back. I can make a poor financial choice sound like an investment opportunity. I've made poor relationship decisions sound like ministry opportunities. I've missed countless workouts under the guise of "I need my rest." I've rationalized gallons of ice cream with the phrase "Everybody needs to live a little," as if ice cream adds to the quality of life. I've wasted massive amounts of time doing all kinds of things that seemed important at the time but had no cumulative value. And given enough time, I can even find a Bible verse or two to support my foolishness.

Every kind of addiction begins with similar self-deception.

"This won't hurt anybody."

"I'll only do it once."

"I haven't had any for a week."

"I'll be careful."

"I can handle it."

"I can quit whenever I want to."

Sound familiar? Chances are, you don't have to think past last week to come up with a bad decision or two that you talked yourself into. Probably some of your greatest regrets started with choices that you convinced yourself were good ones. But in fact you were actually robbing yourself. Your bad choices ended up costing you relationally, financially, and maybe even spiritually.

And the strange thing is, most of the time we are fully aware of the game we're playing. The fact that we have to give ourselves a reason or excuse at all ought to tip us off. Think about it. You don't have to go through a series of mental gymnastics to convince yourself that it's a good idea to eat a serving or two of vegetables every day. You never have to rationalize why you ought to exercise, save money, or avoid bad company. You just know. You don't sit around looking for reasons to do the right thing; it's the bad decisions that require creative reasoning.

READING THE GAUGES

It is this human habit of self-deception that makes the Best Question Ever so uncomfortable to ask. This question exposes the irrationality of our excuses. It reveals our true intent. It penetrates the walls of rationalization behind which we are prone to hide. It dismantles the arguments we use to keep the truth at arm's length.

All of which is fine if you really want to do what is right. But this little question can become a nuisance on those occasions when, instead of trying to make a right decision, you are trying to make a decision right. On those occasions the Best Question Ever has the potential to irritate as well as illuminate. Because of that, it is very important for you to pay close attention to your emotional response to the Best Question Ever. Your reaction to this dynamic little question will tell you a great deal about yourself. And this is one lesson you cannot afford to miss.

3

THE SLIPPERY SLOPE

Why Everybody Goes There

L et me take you now to those verses that altered forever the way I make decisions. We find them in the apostle Paul's first-century letter to Christians residing in the city of Ephesus. You know it as the book of Ephesians.

The letter opens with an inspiring reminder of the believer's new identity that resulted from being adopted into the family of God. For three chapters the author expounds on all the benefits of being "in Christ." Beginning in chapter four, however, Paul turns a corner.

He begins the second half of the book with this plea: "[I] urge you to walk in a manner worthy of the calling to which you have been called" (Ephesians 4:1, ESV). In other words, live your life in a way that reflects the changes God has made in you. Or as a friend of mine is fond of saying, "Don't live the way you used to live. After all, you are not the person you used to be."

From there Paul launches into one of the most practical sections in the Bible. He talks about everything from sex to marriage to alcohol to…you name it. He gives instructions on what is permissible to talk about, think about, and even laugh about. The entire discussion is intense and thorough and, frankly, somewhat overwhelming.

GIMME TRACTION

Paul goes so far as to suggest that we become imitators of God! My gut response? *Yeah, right. Not in this lifetime.*

It's not that Paul's list of lofty standards isn't worth striving toward. It's just that I know me. I'm not that good, that consistent, that disciplined. Besides, just about everything in Paul's list runs directly against the cultural current. So let's face it, I'm not going to get any support out in the real world.

Read Ephesians 4 and 5 for yourself. It's an incredible catalog of virtues and values, the kind of stuff parents preach to their children all the time. But is it realistic? Can anybody really pull it off? At first glance, I think not.

The good news is that Paul anticipates the frustration of his readers. So he incorporates into this intimidating list of what-to-do an invaluable *how-to-do-it*. Specifically, he unveils an approach to life that, if embraced, will set us up for success as we attempt to live out the values he listed. And it is from this short but powerful piece of instruction that we derive the Best Question Ever.

Here's what Paul writes:

Therefore be careful how you walk, not as unwise men but as wise, making the most of your time, because the days are evil. So then do not be foolish, but understand what the will of the Lord is. (Ephesians 5:15–17)

Life changing, huh?

No? Okay, let's break it down.

Paul starts off with a big transition word, a word loaded with implications:

Therefore ...

As a mentor of mine was fond of saying, whenever you see a *therefore*, you gotta ask, "What's it *there for*?" On this particular occasion, "therefore" connects all the stuff Paul is telling us we *need* to do with his explanation of *how* to do it. It's as if he is saying, "If the values and practices I've outlined, as overwhelming as they may seem, are things you desire to embrace, if something in you stirred when you imagined living out those standards, if you want to live life on an entirely different plane, then here's what you need to do."

Then Paul reveals the principle that gives all of us wannabe Christ followers the traction we need to live out what, at times, seems out of reach:

... be careful how you walk...

Or to turn it around, *Don't be careless how you walk.* In other words, following Christ is not a casual endeavor. It requires extreme caution. If we are serious about living out the values the New Testament teaches, we must watch our step. After all, we know from experience how easy it is to stumble.

Then without so much as a pause, Paul discloses the criterion by which we are to measure and judge every one of our choices. In the six words that follow, we are given the grid through which we are to evaluate every invitation and opportunity. Here is the standard, the yardstick by which we are to assess our financial, relational, and professional decisions. Get out your highlighter.

... not as unwise men but as wise...

The Best Question Ever, the question that sets us up for success where it counts, the question that enables us to consistently apply the commands of the New Testament is this:

What is the wise thing to do?

Wait a minute. How could *that* possibly be the Best Question Ever? How could that simplistic question be the key to consistency in our walk with Christ? To understand the potency of this question, we need to examine the way we're used to evaluating our options.

WE'RE ASKING THE WRONG QUESTIONS

Typically when making choices, we run our options and opportunities through a more generic and far less helpful grid. There are several variations, but basically the question we ask ourselves is this: *Is there anything wrong with it?*

The assumption is that if there is nothing *wrong* with what we're doing, it must be okay. If it is not illegal, unethical, or immoral, then it qualifies as a live option, right? Biblically speaking, if there is not a "Thou shalt not" associated with it, then it's safe to assume it qualifies as a "Thou certainly shalt if thou please."

Unfortunately, that kind of thinking sets us up for another question that we rarely verbalize or even allow to surface to the level of conscious thought. Yet if we are honest, this is a question that drives far too many of our choices. It goes something like this: *How close can I get to the line between right and wrong without actually doing something wrong?* The Christian version goes like this: *How close can I get to sin without actually sinning?*

This is a question every teenage guy has asked in some way at some point in his dating career. It's a question everyone on a diet asks every day. It is a question attorneys make a living asking on behalf of their clients.

But it doesn't stop there. Inevitably, once we have come this far we find ourselves asking, *How far over the line between right and wrong can I go without experiencing consequences?* In other words, how unethical, immoral, or insensitive can I be without suffering any unmanageable outcomes? How long can I neglect my family, finances, or professional responsibilities without feeling the effects? How far over the speed limit can I drive without getting pulled over? How far can I indulge in an addictive behavior without actually becoming addicted?

It is a slippery slope, both subtle and sinister. It all begins so innocently by asking what seems to be a noble question, *Is there anything wrong with it?* But it ultimately leads to yet another question. One we have all asked at one time or another: *How did I get myself into this mess?*

DAMAGE CONTROL

It's a question I have heard dozens of times. Heck, I've asked myself the same question a dozen times or more. How in the world could someone as smart and biblically astute as me get myself into—well, it's really none of your business what I've gotten myself into. Let's talk about you, or Frank.

Frank is one of smartest guys I've ever met. Unfortunately, by the time I met him he was attempting to navigate through a labyrinth of sexual addictions, bankruptcy, divorce, and a child custody battle. For forty-five minutes he poured out his heart. He told me about how he and his wife met: He saw the warning signs but ignored them. He told me about his business partner: Again, he saw red flags but moved ahead anyway. He described his early experiences with pornography: He knew the dangers but figured he would be the exception.

Every bad choice Frank had made could have been avoided if only he had asked the Best Question Ever. His was not an IQ problem. As is the case with most people, his nightmare began with the assumption that he could dance on the edge of moral, relational, and professional disaster and beat the odds. If it wasn't technically "wrong" then it must be "right." Right?

Frank is now in the process of rebuilding his life and marriage. He's asking a different set of questions these days. Things are better. But his new perspective can't erase the pain he has caused his wife and daughter. Hopefully, in time, they will trust him again.

As a pastor, I've heard more than my fair share of heart-breaking stories. Yet every bad decision I have ever heard about could have been avoided if someone had simply asked the Best Question Ever. Every single one. Adultery, addictions, unwanted pregnancies, bankruptcies, you name it. All could have been avoided with a proper application of the Best Question Ever.

The moral of the story is, just because there isn't a "Thou shalt not" attached to a situation does not necessarily mean it is a "Thou shalt." What's morally and culturally permissible is often not what's best for us.

Like a good father, God wants what's best for each of us. So He has given us a standard that goes beyond the cultural norms. He has given us a question that enables us to live out the values that lead to what Jesus referred to as an abundant life (see John 10:10). Not a barely-get-by life. Not a life of regret. *An abundant life.*

But the question He gave us is not, *Is there anything wrong with it?* The question is, *Is it the wise thing to do?* To foolproof your life, you must ask it of every invitation, every opportunity, every relationship.

What is the wise thing for me to do?

Think back for a moment to your biggest regret. That event or chapter of your life you wish you could go back and undo or relive. What was the decision you wish you could reverse? The relationship you wish you could do over? Can you see how some or all of what you regret could have been avoided if you had asked and applied the Best Question Ever?

From this moment on, you can avoid the mistakes of the past and live regret free by making it the habit of your life to ask the Best Question Ever.

4

CLIMATE CONTROL

It's a Myth

Our heavenly Father never intended for us to live life at the level of what's permissible, legal, acceptable, and not prosecutable. To do so is tantamount to organizing our lives around the question, *How close can I get to sin without sinning?* Now *there's* a standard.

Instead, we are meant to analyze every opportunity and invitation through the lens of wisdom. Every choice should be tested with the Best Question Ever: *What is the wise thing to do?* This is what Paul was getting at when he admonished us to be careful how we live.

Speaking of Paul, in the last chapter we cut him off in midsentence, so let's pick up where we left off. After telling his audience to walk wisely, Paul goes on to say:

> *...making the most of your time, because the days are evil.*

Evil days? I guess some things never change. If you visit the ruins of Ephesus you can still see phallic symbols etched in the stone walkways, marking the path to the pagan temple. The temple was supported through prostitution. In fact, sex was an integral part of the pagan worship rituals. Drunkenness was encouraged as well. So as you might imagine, the men of Ephesus were religious zealots. *Nobody* missed worship. And it wasn't the music or the preaching that drew the crowds.

Apparently, some of the Christians in Ephesus were being drawn back into their former ways. Why settle for a sermon when you can…never mind. Anyway, they were attempting to blend the old with the new. They were blurring the lines. And some were beginning to suffer the consequences of their actions. So Paul goes right to the heart of the matter.

"You can't be careless!" he warns. "You don't live in a morally neutral environment. If you aren't on your guard, the culture will sweep you right back into the chaos from which you have been rescued."

Asleep at the Wheel

We don't live in a morally neutral climate, either. Every day we interface with a culture of sensuality, gluttony, and greed. Ours is a culture that encourages us in the most provocative ways to do everything in our power to try and satisfy appetites that can never be fully and finally satisfied.

These are evil days. Gone are the days when you had to go looking for trouble. Trouble is on every street corner, on every page of just about every magazine. Trouble is dripping from every billboard. Trouble drives across our television screens and calls to us from our computers.

0% Financing!

The titles of the movies you select will not be listed on your bill.

Buy one, get one free!

Mortgage rates are lower than ever!

Try it for 30 days risk-free!

Girls Gone Wild!

Most Americans are overweight and overleveraged. We eat too much and spend too much. By far, the biggest on-line moneymaker is pornography. Consider this: American men spend hundreds of millions of dollars every year to look at pictures of women on their computer screens. *Hundreds of millions of dollars.*

We do not live in a morally neutral environment. The world we live in is much like the grassy area outside my basement door where I let my black lab, Shadow, out to do her business every night. If you are not "careful how you walk," you will step in it.

That's a little gross, but you get the point. Like the Ephesians in Paul's day, we live in morally and ethically perilous times. The days are evil. If you don't pay attention, you will end up paying a price for your carelessness. If you aren't intentionally cautious, you may end up unintentionally corralled by some vice you've always condemned. If you don't filter your choices through the Best Question Ever, you will find yourself face-to-face with consequences that could have been, and should have been, avoided.

THIS IS YOUR WAKE-UP CALL

I know the question is irritating. After all, it forces you to face up to what you have spent years of time and energy trying to ignore. It's like an alarm clock for your heart, a wake-up call for your soul. It's irritating, but necessary. Perhaps it was the universal propensity to wear out our snooze buttons that drove the apostle Paul to continue with these words:

So then do not be foolish...

If punctuation had been available in the first century, I imagine that this phrase may have come with double exclamation points. "Do not be foolish" is a polite way of saying, "Don't be a fool! Don't approach life as if you lived in a morally and ethically neutral environment!"

Then Paul commands us to do something that on the surface appears to be impossible.

...but understand what the will of the Lord is.

You can't command someone to understand something, can you? I had a Greek teacher in college who would have us come up to the front of the room and translate out loud for the class. There I was with my paperback copy of *The Iliad*, standing in front of my peers and bluffing my way through some incident in the Trojan War, filling in the gaps with my own editorial comments. When it became evident that I was no longer translating but merely telling the story from memory, the teacher would stop me and say, "Mr. Andy, I don't think you are reading." Busted.

"You are right, Mrs. Cuntz," I would reply. "I can't translate it."

Her reply was always the same. "Yes, you can! Now translate it for us."

"I really can't."

"Yes, you can. Now translate."

She would always insist that we understood more than we did, as if her insistence would somehow increase our capacity for the Greek language. It never did. Eventually she would allow us to give up and return to our seats. I always felt like Mrs. Cuntz took my ignorance personally. Funny, it never seemed to bother me. Oh, well.

Whenever I read Paul's admonition to "understand what the will of the Lord is," I always think of Mrs. Cuntz exhorting us to *understand* Plato. Both seem like a waste of time. You can rah-rah an athlete to perform better, but you can't rah-rah someone into knowing something they don't know.

So what is Paul's point? Why didn't he say, *"Discover* what the will of the Lord is"? Or perhaps *"Obey* the will of the Lord"? We could move on either of those. But why *understand?*

FACE-OFF

Paul's command to "understand" God's will is really an exhortation to *face up to* what we know in our hearts God would have us do. As I mentioned earlier, people are masters in the art of self-deception. So Paul, leveraging the grammar of his day, reaches off the page, grabs us by the collar, yanks us up close and shouts, "Quit playing games! Quit pretending, quit rationalizing, ask the question, and embrace the answer!" This is Paul's final attempt to get us to admit what we know in our hearts to be true—to admit that we generally know already what God would have us do.

One reason we don't admit certain things to ourselves is that it helps us to avoid the guilt that naturally follows from not doing what we know we should. This is why most Americans eat so unhealthily. It's not *just* a lack of discipline. Americans haven't really faced up to the reality of what the foods they eat are doing to their bodies. How do I know? Because I've seen how quickly the diet changes once someone has had a brush with cancer or heart disease. Lumps, clogs, and shortness of breath force a person to face up to what he or she has refused to acknowledge for years. And the revelation leads to death-defying discipline.

But lifestyle changes don't happen until an individual faces the facts. It is not until a person acknowledges the truth and quits lying to himself that something positive takes place. And once someone has turned the corner mentally, it's amazing how quickly that person is able to break unhealthy habits and begin new routines.

Every person I know who has undergone this kind of transformation after a health scare says the same thing: "I should have made these changes years ago."

Translated: "For years I refused to face up to what I knew in my heart was true."

Bankruptcy can have the same effect. So can an unwanted pregnancy, a letter from your spouse's attorney, a DUI, or a trip to detox with one of your kids. And perhaps that's what it will take. There is something out there somewhere that has the ability to get your attention. Unfortunately, that something may scar you as well as scare you. You may be left with limited options and reduced opportunities. So why let things go that far? Why not face up now to what you know in your heart your heavenly Father wants you to do?

Why not start asking the Best Question Ever?

5

STEMMING
THE TIDE

Avoiding the Undertow

When I was a kid we lived in Miami. Every summer we would pull our eighteen-foot travel trailer to Naples, Florida, for a week of vacation. If you've been to Naples lately, you know the waterfront is lined with condos and hotels. But in 1968 there was nothing but miles of empty beach. So my dad would actually pull out onto the beach and drive along the tree line where the sand was firm. Then we would drive for miles until we found a suitable place to set up camp.

Although I was in elementary school at the time, I still have a vivid memory of something that happened during one of our weeks on the beach. That particular year the undertow was ferocious. It wasn't dangerous, in the sense that the undertow might pull you out to sea, but it would carry you down the beach in no time. I still remember playing in the water, looking back toward the shore, and our trailer not being there! Why would my parents move the campsite? Well, of course, they hadn't moved—I was forty yards down the beach from where I had stepped into the water. It was the undertow.

Well, after a couple of days of looking out from the trailer and wondering where his kids had drifted off to, my dad came up with a novel idea. He gathered about twenty coconuts and made a neat little cannonball-like stack about thirty yards down the beach from where our trailer was parked. The coconuts were to serve as a reference point. Once we drifted past the coconuts we were to get out of the water, walk back to the point where we were even with the trailer, and then we could swim again. And it worked.

You may already know where I'm going with this. Like the undertow at Naples, culture has a way of subtly sweeping us beyond healthy moral, ethical, and financial limits. That accounts for the times when we have looked up and said, "Who moved the trailer?" Or rather, "How did I get myself into this situation?" When everything around you is drifting along at the same rate, it's easy to be fooled into thinking that you're standing still. Without a stationary reference point, it is impossible to ascertain where you are, where you aren't, and where you ought to be.

So let's stake out some stationary reference points.

Specifically, we are going to ask the Best Question Ever in three different ways. Each version of the question will provide you with a unique perspective on the choices you are currently making. Approaching the question from three different angles will provide you with a point of reference that will give you valuable, if not bothersome, insight into where you are and where you are headed.

Ready?

Here we go.

Looking Back

Poet and philosopher George Santayana once said, "Those who cannot remember the past are condemned to repeat it." On a personal level that axiom could be restated this way: "Those who don't pay attention to what got them into trouble yesterday are liable to end up in the same trouble tomorrow."

It's not very catchy, but you get the point.

We have about a zillion singles in our church. Many come to faith as a result of the brokenness associated with unsuccessful relationships. In his or her own way, each of these people comes asking the question, "Why does every relationship end the same way?" In most cases the answer is, "Because every relationship started the same way."

I wonder if Dr. Laura is looking for a cohost?

Not only did every relationship start the same way, they were conducted the same way as well. So consequently, they all ended the same way. We mistakenly think that swapping partners will itself guarantee us a different kind of relation-ship. It's the same line of thinking that leads us to buy new tennis rackets, golf clubs, and baseball bats—as if new equip-ment will somehow compensate for a poor swing. Expensive cookware does not necessarily result in gourmet cooking. A new guitar does not guarantee better music. And bad rela-tional habits are not corrected by starting a new relationship.

So the Best Question Ever needs to be asked with an eye to the rearview mirror: *In light of your past experience, what is the wise thing to do?*

History Lessons

Your personal history is unique to you. And the sum of your past experiences predisposes you toward specific weaknesses and strengths in your relationships, finances, career, etc. For example, your personal history makes you more prone to temptation in some areas than in others. Consequently, what's safe for some folks may not be safe for you. There are activities that others find it easy to walk away from while you are prone to overindulge. So every decision, invitation, and opportunity that comes your way needs to be filtered through this question: In light of my past experience, what's the wise thing to do?

I have a friend who received some startling advice when he went through premarital counseling with his fiancée. The counselor told him, "You come from such a dysfunctional family that, when you return from your honeymoon, you need to come back in to see me."

My friend was shocked. The counselor continued. "We need to spend about six months just working through the stuff you're bringing into this relationship. It isn't marriage problems I'm concerned about; it's the *you* problems that will impact the marriage."

Now, most people don't continue premarital counseling after the wedding. Most couples don't get *any* counseling before they say, "I do." So my buddy had every right to ask Dr. Encouragement how often he required postnuptial visits from his premarital counselees and take his cue from there. But instead, a month after returning from his honeymoon, my friend went back for another round of counseling. Why? Not because it was standard operating procedure. Not because of a verse of Scripture. Not because of a universal moral or ethical imperative. He went back because in light of his past experience, it was the *wise thing* for him to do.

It was a decision my friend never regretted. And it spoke volumes to his new wife about his commitment to their marriage.

Your past experience must be a grid through which you evaluate every decision. Chances are, there are places you have no business visiting because of your history—places that would have no impact on the average person, but the average person doesn't share your experience with those environ-

ments. Perhaps there are certain types of people you have no business spending time with. Being around them triggers something unhealthy in you. I have a good friend who was once active in the gay community. Although he walked away from that lifestyle years ago, he knows there are certain types of people that it's not good for him to be around.

I have another friend who tried numerous times unsuccessfully to break free from that lifestyle. Jake fell back into his same patterns time and again because he refused to break his ties with his old friends. His excuse was always the same: "But Andy, if I walk away, who's going to reach out to my gay friends?"

My answer was always the same, too: "Somebody other than you!"

Then Jake would quote Scripture to me about loving the unlovable and laying down one's life for a friend. His intentions were good. But in light of his past experience, it was terribly unwise for him to continue to interact with men who shared his weakness. Jake had to learn the hard way. After an experience that nearly cost him his life, he made his break. Nine years ago, Jake married a wonderful girl he met on a singles retreat. He would be the first to admit that apart from the Best Question Ever he would have never been able to break free.

I know people who refuse to buy on credit because of their past experience with credit cards. Is there anything inherently wrong with a credit card? I hope not. I use one all

the time. But for those people whose pasts are cluttered with financial problems due to their unwise use of credit, it is wise to stay away.

I know guys who got rid of their satellite dishes. Women who canceled their Internet connections. Singles who quit dating for a season. All because of the Best Question Ever.

These are men and women who had the courage to face up to God's will for their lives. They knew that their past set them up for failure if they did not take drastic steps. So in light of their past experience, they did the wise thing. The unusual thing. The extreme thing.

GUT CHECK

What about you? In light of your past experience, what is the wise thing for *you* to do?

What is the wise thing for you to do financially?

Professionally?

Relationally?

Where are you set up to fail because of something in your past? Perhaps it was something you had no control over, yet there it is, reaching into your current experience and wreaking havoc with your choices. Does the way you were raised predispose you to an area of temptation to which most people seem immune? If so, admit it. Own up to it. Don't be content with merely doing the right thing. *Do the wise thing.*

6

SEASONAL WISDOM

Biding Your Time

I have suggested that asking the Best Question Ever from three different perspectives will provide you with a point of reference, giving you valuable insight into where you are and where you are headed. Here's the second form of the question.

In light of my current circumstances, what is the wise thing to do?

Life is seasonal. Today's sorrow will be replaced by tomorrow's joy. Today's anger will probably be tempered with tomorrow's perspective. Today's worry will be replaced by tomorrow's concerns. As Jesus taught, each day has its own worries. If we are not careful, we will allow the pressure, fears, and circumstances of today drive us to make decisions we will regret tomorrow.

That being the case, you owe it to yourself, and to the people you love, to take your current emotions and state of mind into account when making decisions. I don't know about you, but most of my apologies stem from my propensity to react to the moment. When the moment has passed, I discover I have overreacted and hurt someone in the process. I can't begin to remember all of the e-mails I wish I could unsend—I know that if I had waited even twenty-four hours my response would have been much different. Consequently, there would have been far less residual damage. When I'm mad, I've learned that the wise thing for me to do is NOTHING. Just wait.

BEYOND THE MOMENT

But this angle on the Best Question Ever goes beyond the moment. What's wise in this season of life may be unwise in the next. And vice versa.

For example, I have no problem with women working outside the home. Our church would cease to function without our incredible female staff. But for some women, during certain stages of their lives, maintaining a career outside the home is not the most prudent thing to do. The question is not, "Should women work outside the home?" Neither is it, "Should a particular woman work outside the home?" The question marketplace moms should ask is, "Is it wise for me to work outside the home during this particular season of life?"

Sandra sold real estate during the first four years of our

marriage. When we had our first child, she came home to be a full-time mom. That was an easy decision. Since then, however, as our children have gotten older, there have been times when we've toyed with the idea of her jumping back into the workforce. This is especially enticing when someone asks her to help them list or find an expensive (read: high commission) home.

But for us, it always comes back to the Best Question Ever. Whereas it may be financially profitable for my wife to jump back into real estate, in light of our current season of life, it would not be the wise thing to do.

No Decision

Every pastor is forced to grapple with issues surrounding divorce and remarriage. I am certainly not immune. As I mentioned, we have several thousand singles in our church, many of them nursing the wounds from a painful divorce. At the same time, these hurting people desire companionship. And more often than not, before the ink is dry on the divorce papers, they are already in a new relationship. And those that aren't in one are looking for one. I imagine I would be the same way.

Now, there's nothing wrong with desiring companionship. There's nothing wrong with moving on with your life once you have closed the door on a difficult chapter. But those aren't really the issues. For single men and women who find themselves in this challenging season of life, the question they must ask is, "In light of what I've just come through, my current state of mind, my frazzled emotions, what is the wise thing to do relationally?"

Dozens of times newly divorced men and women have asked me what I think about remarriage. I give everybody the same advice. I tell them to pull out their calendars and mark the day one year from today. Then I tell them not to make any decisions or even form an opinion about remarriage for a year. Why? Because in light of their current reality, it is usually unwise to try to make that kind of decision. Some people take my advice, and of those, many have written to thank me. Most people think I'm too extreme. Some of them have had the courage to write and tell me they wish they had listened. A handful of people actually make appointments to come in with their new spouses and get advice about how to rescue their second marriages. I never say, "I told you so." But I certainly think it.

I feel so strongly about this that I have asked our pastors not to perform second marriages for individuals who have been divorced for less then two years. Do I have a verse to support this policy? Nope. Is it wrong to remarry before two years has passed? That's not the issue. It all goes back to the Best Question Ever: What is the wise thing to do? I've never had anyone attribute their marriage problems to the fact that they waited too long to marry. But I've talked to countless folks who wish they had waited longer.

Look Around

So in light of what's going on in your life right now, what is the wise thing for you to do? As you consider your frame of mind, your emotional state, and even your physical health, what is the wise thing to do? As you consider your current responsibilities and commitments, things that a year from now may not be a factor, what is the wise thing to do? As you examine the current status of your finances, what is the wise thing to do?

Life is seasonal. What is appropriate today may be completely inappropriate a month from now. What is foolish today may be prudent tomorrow. It is not enough to determine what is legal, permissible, or even practical. As a Christ-follower you have been called to approach life with a different standard. So you must ask, "For me, in light of my past experience and my current season of life, what is the wise thing to do?"

7

LOOKING AHEAD

Creating a Preferred Future

The Best Question Ever will provide you with the greatest insight when asked from three different angles. Again, each form of the question will provide you with a unique perspective on your options and decisions. Here's the final version of the question:

In light of my future hopes and dreams, what is the wise thing to do?

No doubt, you have a mental picture of how you want your future to look. It may be general. It may be scripted out in detail. You may have gone to the effort of writing it down, complete with incremental steps and artificial deadlines. While certain personalities are driven to slave over their goals and objectives, others are content to simply dream. Either way, everybody has a mental picture of how they want their future to pan out. A mental image of what could and should be.

If I were to ask you where you envision yourself in ten years financially, you could come up with an answer. You have some idea of what that should look like. You may not have a plan for getting there, but you almost certainly have a mental picture of what you would like the future to look like financially. If you were pressed to describe your future relationally or professionally, you could come up with a general description for those aspects of your life as well. We all have certain hopes and dreams for the future. We may lack a plan, but we certainly have dreams and expectations.

DREAM WRECKERS

The truth is, most people's dreams don't come true. I don't know too many adults who are living their dream. And while it is true that the twists and turns of life can reshape our future, that is not the primary reason people are robbed of their dreams. We rob ourselves. We rob ourselves when we make decisions in the moment with no thought of how these decisions will impact our future.

This is easy to see in others. But somehow the man or woman in the mirror is always the exception, or so we think.

You know people who have robbed themselves of their preferred future. Too much debt, too much alcohol, too many risks, too many relationships, too many nights out, too many missed classes. We have all watched somebody we care about trade his or her dreams for a moment, a weekend, a habit, a promise, or a kiss.

As a parent I am constantly urging my kids to make today's decisions in light of tomorrow's hopes and dreams. The future is what brings today's choices into proper focus. Making choices with the end in mind goes a long way toward ensuring a happy ending.

Today's decisions must be evaluated in light of how they will impact and shape tomorrow. Short of winning the lottery, your financial future will be determined by today's financial decisions. The health of your marriage tomorrow will be determined by the decisions you make today. The nature of my relationship with my children once they are grown and gone hinges in large part on the decisions I make while they are still living at home.

I was reminded of the significance of this principle recently as I listened to a brokenhearted father describe his failed attempts to reconnect with his adult daughter. He could not understand why she refused to return his calls or accept his gifts. She was now married and had a little girl of her own. In her father's words, she was "depriving him" of his rights to be the grandfather he had always dreamed of being. From where he stood, she had shut him out of her life for good, and with no justification. He was devastated.

But that wasn't the whole story.

When his daughter turned twelve, this man was in the third year of an affair with an employee. His wife knew what was going on but could never prove it. On many occasions she would drive around their small town, looking for his car.

Their daughter was with her mom the night she spotted his car in a hotel parking lot at the edge of town. This twelve-year-old girl saw her father come out of the room with his girlfriend in tow. She endured the humiliation that accompanied the divorce proceedings. And then she didn't hear from her father for fifteen years.

As much as I empathized with a father who wanted a relationship with his only daughter, I couldn't help but think, *You did this to yourself. You robbed yourself of the joy of seeing your daughter graduate from high school. You missed the once-in-a-lifetime opportunity to give her away at her wedding. You weren't there for the birth of your granddaughter.* One stupid, irresponsible decision robbed him of what could have been and what should have been.

But he wasn't the only person whose dreams wouldn't come true. His daughter certainly didn't imagine growing up without her father. His wife certainly didn't dream of becoming a single mom. His decision derailed the dreams of everyone who was close to him. The shrapnel of his choices wounded everyone who loved him. In a moment, the future was changed forever. Nobody's dreams would come true.

FUTURE TENSE, COMMON SENSE

Asking the Best Question Ever with the future in mind casts a trenchant light on the validity of our options. The deceptive shades of gray dissipate. The nature of the journey on which we are about to embark becomes painfully clear. So clear that we are tempted to look away, to retreat to the often-rehearsed excuses that have buttressed our misguided decisions for years: *I'm not doing anything wrong. People do it all the time. I'm not hurting anyone. I can handle it. There's no law against it. Nobody's going to find out. Nothing's going to happen.*

Recently, the director of our student ministry asked each of our high school students to write a letter to his or her future spouse. The response was amazing. For most of the students this was the first time they had given their undivided attention to what they were looking forward to relationally. In a defining moment, it dawned on these young people how their current behavior would be either an investment in or a deterrent to that future relationship.

Following the letter-writing exercise, the leaders enacted a mock wedding, and our students were transported to an event so far in the future that it seemed to have no connection to the realities of their everyday lives. But in that moment, when they were fast-forwarded to a marriage altar with all it represents, the casual decisions of adolescence took on extraordinary meaning. Suddenly, they realized that their tomorrows would, in fact, be shaped by today. The decisions made at thirteen could sculpt what life looked like at thirty-one.

The students were not the only ones moved by this exercise. Our adult leaders were impacted as well. But as you can imagine, their takeaway was somewhat different from that of the students. Their response: "I wish someone had helped me to stop and think about my decisions based on how they would affect me in the future." Most of us had someone in our lives who tried. But we were seventeen and knew everything.

But the fact that the adults would feel that way should tell you something very important about all of us: Our lives would be better today if we had been asking the Best Question Ever along the way. We might be closer to living our dreams if we had guarded them more closely.

Is it too late to begin viewing today through the lens of tomorrow? I don't think so. Chances are, you've got plenty of tomorrows left.

So that settles it, right? From now on you will gauge the appropriateness of every option by your hopes and dreams for tomorrow. Every time there is a decision to make, you will reflexively stop and ask, "In light of my future hopes and dreams, what is the wise thing to do?" And then you will do it!

End of story. No need to finish this book.

Maybe Not

It's not that simple, is it? Or is it? Seems strange that we would digest this information and then turn right around and resist the obvious.

Isn't it ironic that at this very moment you are seriously contemplating a decision that has the potential to chip away at your preferred future, and yet you are leaning hard in that direction, rehearsing the same old worn-out excuses? You know which ones I'm talking about. The ones you've been using since high school. The ones that cleared the way for you to do things you now wish you hadn't. Things you have never shared with your spouse. Things you hope your children never discover. Decisions you are ashamed of…choices that, to this day, cast a shadow over the good things that have come your way. Options that, if avoided, would have paved the way for your dreams to come true.

Sorry to be so hard on you. It's just that I know my own tendency to deny this truth in the face of overwhelming evidence to the contrary. As I said earlier, it's easy to see how this principle has played out in the lives of others while ignoring its relevance in our own lives. We are a people proficient in the art of self-deception.

So let's get specific. In light of where you want to be financially in ten years, what's the wise thing to do right now? What do you need to start or stop doing financially?

If you are single, in hopes of one day finding the man or woman of your dreams, what is the wise way to conduct your relationships now? What are you doing that has the potential to rob you of your preferred future? What do you want to tell your future spouse about your past relationships? Live accordingly. If you are married and your dream is to finish life together with your spouse, what options do you need to take off the table? What's out there that could steal your dream? What precautions need to be taken? What's the wise thing to do relationally?

In light of how you envision your relationship with your children when they're teenagers or in college or married with children of their own, what is the wise thing to do now? What practices would you be wise to incorporate now into your parenting repertoire? Where do you need to reprioritize?

It would be nice if we could go back and redo adolescence. Oh, and maybe drop in and redo some chapters from our twenties and thirties. But, of course, we can't. We only get one shot at every season of life. Whether or not we learned anything becomes evident in the seasons that follow.

So what have you learned? More to the point, are you willing to face up to God's will for your life? Are you ready to acknowledge what you know in your heart is true? Are you prepared to ask the Best Question Ever and follow through? Take a giant step toward protecting your future. In light of your future hopes and dreams, what is the wise thing to do?

Where Does It Hurt?

For just a moment, let's pretend that no one, including God, can read your mind. Better yet, let's imagine that five minutes from now you will be able to erase your next five minutes' worth of thoughts. In other words, let's create some space for unfiltered thinking. You will not be accountable to anyone, including yourself, for the thoughts you are about to entertain.

If you can go with this for just a minute, you will be free to admit to yourself anything you want without feeling like you have to do anything about it. Because in five minutes you will be able to erase any incriminating thoughts that you allow yourself to think. With me?

Okay, let's do a little probing. Remember, you are free to admit to yourself anything you want. No action will be required.

As you evaluate where you are financially, relationally, morally, professionally, and spiritually, what would you do differently in each of these areas if you were to embrace the Best Question Ever? In light of your past experience, current circumstances, and future hopes and dreams, what is the wise thing to do financially? Relationally? Morally? Professionally? Spiritually?

Again, you don't have to act on your answers. Just take a moment to be painfully honest with yourself. What would you do differently in each of these areas if you were to evaluate each component of your life through the lens of the Best Question Ever?

Remember, you're not asking this question for anybody but yourself. What's the wise thing *for me* to do? Resist the temptation to hide behind broad generalities and cultural norms. What is the wise thing for *you* to do? You are a unique blend of past experiences, current circumstances, and future hopes and dreams. Wisdom allows you to customize the decision-making process to your specific professional, financial, and relational dimensions. Don't miss this opportunity.

Think about how different your life would be now if you had been processing your options this way from the beginning. Imagine how different your life might look a year from now if you embraced the Best Question Ever from this point forward.

Okay, back to the real world. No need to feel guilty about what you just admitted to yourself but don't intend to do anything about. We've got several more chapters to wear down your resistance.

In the next section we are going to drill down a little further into a few of the areas we referred to throughout this section. Specifically, we are going to apply the Best Question Ever to the worlds of finance, morality, and time.

Part II

A QUESTION
OF TIME

8

TIME BANDITS

Having the Time of Your Life

When it comes to asking the Best Question Ever, there is no more crucial arena than that of *time*. Your time equals your life. You can run out of money and still have some life left. You can run out of friends with life to spare. But once you run out of time, it's over.

If there is one commodity we must learn to handle wisely, it is our time. Think about it. You can make more money, make new friends, take more trips, maybe even have another child. But your allotment of time is inflexible. You only get so much of it. Job put it this way:

> Man's days are determined; you have decreed the number of his months and have set limits he cannot exceed. (Job 14:5, NIV)

Did you catch those last four words? "Limits he cannot exceed." You can overspend, overeat, and overachieve, but you can't "overlive."

The psalmist adds this insight regarding the relationship between our allotment of time and wisdom:

Teach us to number our days aright, that we may gain a heart of wisdom. (Psalm 90:12, NIV)

I love that verse. Simply by recognizing that our days are numbered we take a giant step towards becoming men and women of wisdom.

Just the sheer recognition that our time on this earth is limited should compel us to evaluate all of life differently. Unfortunately, we spend more of our lives asking for the time than evaluating how well we're investing it. But as we are about to discover, there's something far more significant than knowing what time it is: It's knowing what to do with our time.

WHICH WAY DID IT GO?

Sandra and I were married for almost five years before we had our first child. When we think back to those days of child-free living, we often wonder, *What in the world did we do with all that extra time?* Shouldn't we have something significant to show for those unencumbered years? Where did all that time go?

The answer: away.

It went *away*. And there is no way to recover a minute of it. There is no leftover time. It can't be saved up for later. You can't store it. It just goes *away*. So we all look back and wonder where the time went. It seems like just yesterday I was sixteen. Where did my twenties go? Why don't I have more to show for my thirties?

When we ask, "Where did the time go?" we are really asking another, more bewildering, question: "Where did my *life* go?" You see, what we do with our time is more important than simply knowing what time it is, how old we are, or even how much time we have left. The fact that time is life and can't be recovered is why we must bring the Best Question Ever to bear on this priceless commodity.

In light of my past experiences, my current responsibilities, and my future hopes and dreams, what is the wisest way to invest my time?

Now, we could end this chapter right here. You are smart enough to objectively evaluate your time commitments and make the necessary adjustments. And you have lived long enough to know that time is life. But before we move on, I would like to dig deeper into one aspect of time that so often eludes us. This is something everybody figures out eventually, but sometimes *eventually* is too late. This is one of those life lessons that, regardless of when we learn it, we wish we had learned it earlier.

CHIPPING AWAY

I will keep this simple because this is actually a very simple principle. I've broken it down into five statements. Here's the first:

> *There is a cumulative value to investing small amounts of time in certain activities over a long period.*

Exercise is an obvious illustration of this principle. There's a clear cumulative effect from exercising a few minutes every day or every other day over a long period of time. At the end of a year, you can see and feel a difference. But at the end of your first exercise session, the only difference is that you are sore. You will see almost no measurable benefit from one exercise session; in fact, no matter how long you have been exercising, there is almost no measurable benefit from a single session. That's why it is so easy to talk ourselves out of exercise. *What will it hurt if I miss one day?* The answer is, it won't hurt anything, physically speaking. The real value in exercise is not found in any one deposit of time; the value is realized at the end of a sequence of deposits. Exercise has a compounding effect. It is the consistent, incremental investments of time that make a difference.

The same is true if you are attempting to master a musical instrument or perfect your golf swing or gain proficiency in the martial arts. A little bit of concentrated effort several days a week over a period of six months will drastically improve your performance.

Now, what is obviously true in the realms of physical fitness and music is not so obvious in other areas; nevertheless, it has implications for just about every facet of our lives, especially those pertaining to relationships. Let me list a few specific practices where consistency will make a difference: dinner with the family, date night with your spouse, time alone with God, church attendance, one-on-one time with your children, praying with your family, small-group Bible study, going to bed at the same time as your spouse. There is no real measurable gain derived from any of these activities if you are keeping score based solely on any individual installment of time.

What's the takeaway from putting your kids to bed one Tuesday night? Occasionally, you might have a significant conversation with one of your children. Or a single evening of Bible study with a small group? On a good night you might gain a new insight from someone in your small group. But for the most part it wouldn't be the end of the world if you did something else with that time. Dinner with the family is, well, it is dinner with the family. What is gained in one installment of time around the dinner table? Not much.

But as a father who eats dinner with his family five or six nights a week, I can tell you that there is cumulative value in that seemingly unimportant routine. As a Christian who was taught early on to open God's Word alone every morning, I can vouch for the cumulative value of those incremental investments of time. And as a couple that has devoted three Monday nights a month to participating in a small group, Sandra and I know the cumulative value of being in community with a handful of other believers.

No specific dinnertime conversation comes to mind. I can't think of a particular discussion with our small group that changed my life. Bedtime conversations with my children are rarely all that productive or memorable. But these routines, these incremental investments of time—life—have immeasurable cumulative value.

And that leads me to my second statement:

> *There are rarely any immediate*
> *consequences for neglecting single installments*
> *of time in any arena of life.*

WHAT'S THE BIG DEAL?

Once again, it is in the realm of our health that we find the clearest example of this maxim. Neglect your health for a day and there are no immediate consequences. Neglect your health for a week and you won't experience any negative effects. In fact, after a week of fast food, double desserts, no exercise, a few too many beers, and several late nights out on the town, you may wonder why you didn't adopt this lifestyle earlier. (Or you may wonder why you gave it up!) If you were to evaluate the effects of such a lifestyle after a single week, you would probably draw some wrong conclusions. Other than a little indigestion and some difficulty getting up in the mornings, there wouldn't seem to be anything to worry about.

This same dynamic plays itself out in every area of life. If you miss dinner with the family one night, it's no big deal. If you choose to sleep in one Sunday morning, nothing changes. Skip work one Friday and you'll probably still have a job on Monday. Pick up a newspaper instead of your Bible one morning and life goes on. It's deceiving but true that we rarely see any immediate consequences for neglecting a single installment of time in any arena of life. But if neglect becomes your pattern, you will eventually bump up against our third principle:

Neglect has a cumulative effect.

You can neglect your health for a week or maybe even a month without any serious consequences. But strap that lifestyle on for ten or twelve years and the damage might be irreversible. Not because of a single night out or one particular meal. The effect is cumulative.

Neglect has a cumulative effect physically, relationally, spiritually, professionally, financially, emotionally, and horticulturally. *Horticulturally*? I just looked out at my lawn. Neglect anything over a long period of time and you will have something to show for it. Usually a mess—a mess that can generate in us a wave of concern and even energy. Suddenly we realize what we have done and we rush out to the yard to reverse the consequences of our neglect.

But in the areas that matter most, a burst of energy and activity cannot reverse the consequences that accompany a season of neglect. More on that a little later.

It Doesn't Add Up

The next stop in our five-point journey is something you have probably never thought about but have certainly experienced. While it is true that small, consistent investments of time add up to *good* things, and that consistent neglect adds up to *bad* things, the random pursuits that we allow to interrupt our important routines add up to *no-thing*:

> *There is no cumulative value to the urgent things that*
> *we allow to interfere with the important things.*

Allow me to illustrate. Let's suppose your New Year's resolution this past January was to exercise three days a week. You joined a health club. You bought a treadmill. You announced to friends and family that this would be your year to get in shape. Now let's imagine that it hasn't worked out: Other things kept interfering with your exercise routine. Chances are, you are not having to use much imagination on this one, but let's take it a step further.

Now imagine that you have to sit down with a friend six months into the year and explain what you did instead of exercising. How might that conversation go?

"What did you do instead of exercising?" she asks.

"Um, I don't know. A lot of things, I guess."

"Well, let's think about it. Did you sleep in a few mornings?"

"Yeah, that's right. Sometimes I got a few extra hours of sleep."

"Okay, how many times?"

"I don't know."

"What else did you do instead of exercising?"

"I went to the office early."

"How many times?"

"I don't know."

"What did you do at the office?"

"Different stuff."

"What stuff?"

"I can't remember. Just stuff. Work stuff."

"Okay. What else did you do with those mornings instead of exercise?

"On a couple of occasions I had breakfast with friends."

"What else?"

"Some mornings I just got up and piddled around the house. Checked my e-mail. Helped get the kids off to school."

Here's the point: If you stack up all the stuff you did instead of exercising, then added up their value, what would you end up with? Zero. The random pursuits that interrupt our important routines don't add up to *anything*. Well, actually, they add up to a lot of wasted time. There's never any cumulative value to all the things we do *instead of* the things we know are truly important.

What's the cumulative value of all the things a college freshman does instead of studying? Zero. What's the cumulative value of all the things a father does instead of having dinner with his family? Zero. What's the cumulative value of all the things that have interfered with your devotional time? Zero.

When random urgent activities constantly interfere with strategic deposits of time, it is like throwing away our most precious commodity. It is worse than wasting time. We waste our life.

This principle explains why we don't have more to show for our time. It all gets gobbled up with random, unquantifiable activities—activities that rob us of what's most important. When you add up all the what-I-did-instead-ofs, they always equal zero.

Before we dive into the fifth and final statement, let's take a look at what we have said so far.

1. There is a cumulative value to investing small amounts of time in certain activities over a long period.
2. There are rarely any immediate consequences for neglecting single installments of time in any arena of life.
3. Neglect has a cumulative effect.
4. There is no cumulative value to the urgent things that we allow to interfere with the important things.

If all of this is true, and time equals life, what is the wise thing to do as it relates to your time?

9

LIVE AND LEARN

Eddie Money Was Right

S urely you remember Eddie Money? Big pop star in the 1980s. Lots of hits. Very cool-looking guy. He usually appeared in still photos with a cigarette perched between his fingers. The reason I bring him up is that one of his biggest hits underscores the searing truth of our fifth and final statement about time. The song is entitled "I Wanna Go Back." The chorus goes something like this:

> *I know that things will never be the same.*
> *I wanna go back*
> *and do it all over again,*
> *but I can't go back, I know.*

Eddie's right. We can't go back. We can't go back and relive, relove, retrieve, rearrange, reprioritize, redirect, or refocus. Looking back, there are times we wanna go back. But we can't. You can't relive your teens, twenties, or thirties. You can't rewind your marriage. You can't reraise your kids. Depressed yet?

Here's my fifth and final statement:

> *In the critical arenas of life,*
> *you cannot make up for lost time.*

As students we could pull an all-nighter to make up for the studying we should have been doing all week. On vacation you can drive a little faster than normal to make up the time lost during your four-year-old's potty break. But in the world of relationships there are no all-nighters. You can't cram for a better relationship with your kids or your spouse. Speeding up doesn't make up for lost time with your heavenly Father. The important areas of life require small deposits *all along the way*. And if you miss those opportunities, they are lost forever.

Most of us have made the mistake of trying to make up for missed time in the gym. You know what I'm talking about. You haven't exercised in years, then suddenly you decide to get back into shape. So what do you do? The MEGAWORKOUT. You strap yourself into every machine in the building. You lift every weight. You log in time on the treadmill, the Lifecycle, the StairMaster, the elliptical. You do it all. You know better, but something in you says, "I can make up for lost time; I can make up for my neglect." And so you walk away convinced that you have reclaimed lost ground. You feel so toned, so in shape. You even consider running for governor.

But the next morning you can't get out of bed. In fact, you are so sore you don't go the gym for a week. Or worse, you injure yourself and are out for even longer. The moral of the story is, you cannot make up for lost time in the areas of life that matter most.

So what is the wise thing to do now?

Dad, it won't do any good to rush home tonight and announce to the family, "It just occurred to me that I've missed too many dinners with the fam. So load up! Tonight, we're going to eat out at *all* our favorite restaurants. We'll go till midnight or later if we have to. We'll eat and eat and eat, and talk and talk and talk. We are making up for lost time."

Ridiculous? Perhaps. But no more ridiculous than thinking a long vacation can make up for being an absentee parent. It is no more ridiculous than promising a romantic weekend getaway to make up for months of work-related travel. A weekend together can't rescue a marriage that's been neglected for six months or more—no matter how romantic you make it.

Relationships are built on small, consistent deposits of time. You can't cram for what's most important. If you want to connect with your kids, you've got to be available consistently, not randomly. A vacation or weekend getaway is a good way to commemorate or celebrate the past or even changes on the horizon. But neither can compensate for consistent neglect.

So, once again, what is the wise thing for you to do?

REDEEMING THE TIME

With these five statements as a backdrop, look once again at Paul's warning to the believers in Ephesus:

> Therefore be careful how you walk, not as unwise men but as wise, *making the most of your time,* because the days are evil. (Ephesians 5:15–16, emphasis mine)

The phrase "making the most of your time" is literally "redeeming the time." The Greek term used here is an accounting term. Paul was saying, "Get the full value out of your time—squeeze all the good you can out of every moment of your life." Misappropriated time is misappropriated life. Be wise. Make the most of your time. You can't go back and reinvest it.

Did you catch the reason Paul gives for redeeming the time? "Because the days are evil."

As we said earlier, we don't live in a morally or ethically neutral environment. As a follower of Christ, your values are constantly being challenged—challenged by another value system. If you aren't on your guard, the culture will draw you into a lifestyle where your time is frivolously consumed rather than strategically invested. You will be busy. You may even be productive. But if you are not being "careful," you will miss those irretrievable opportunities to make small, incremental time deposits in the things that matter most. If you are not walking wisely, your time will be fragmented by a thousand urgent, disconnected opportunities and events. Such opportunities and events will seem important at the time, but when strung together they have no cumulative value.

But if you are willing to harness your time and appropriate it strategically, things can be different. You will be healthier physically, relationally, spiritually, and possibly, financially. You will look back at this next season of life with few, if any, regrets. Not because of a single day or a single burst of activity, but because of a single decision: the decision to get full value out of your time by making small, incremental investments of time in the things that matter most.

STUDIO TIME CAN BE EXPENSIVE

So in the light of your past, your present, and your future hopes and dreams, what needs to change about the way you are spending your time? What do you need to stop doing? What do you need to cancel? Chances are, the things that come to mind are not *bad* things. But remember, we have been called to a higher standard. What is the *wise* thing to do with your time? What in your current schedule is distracting you from making incremental investments of time in what's most important?

The biggest test I have ever faced in this area came a decade ago, right after Garrett, our second son, was born. I love music. In the early days of my marriage, I had a little music studio in our condo, along with a lot of gear that I had started accumulating when I was single. Marriage certainly cut into my studio time, but I continued to find a few hours here and there to disappear into my private world of music. When our first son, Andrew, was born, I found it increasingly difficult to carve out time for music. Sandra was very understanding and encouraged me to take whatever time I could find to pursue my musical interest.

Right after Garrett was born, we moved into a larger rental house. I was in the basement hooking up all my stuff one night when suddenly a thought hit me: *You know, Andy, you're about to invest another big block of your life in something that is fun but not very productive, and upstairs are the three people you love the most and two of them are in diapers.* As I sat there thinking about the future, I knew that one day I would look back and wish I had invested more time with the people I loved than with the hobby I loved. I knew that the block of time—life—I would invest in music would be better spent with my family.

I went upstairs and announced to Sandra that I wasn't

even going to set my studio up, but instead I was going to sell everything. She was both shocked and relieved. In spite of her patience and encouragement, I knew there were times when she felt like she had to compete for my attention.

Looking back, that was one of the best decisions I ever made. There was nothing wrong with having a music studio, but in light of my desire to stay meaningfully connected to my family, giving it up was the wise thing for me to do. Do I miss my music? Sometimes. But I have never second-guessed my decision. And ten years later, I am still enjoying the dividends from that simple decision. Besides, I can't imagine adding a time-consuming hobby to my already-packed schedule. But hey, that's just me. The question is, what is the wise thing for *you* to do?

I'm not suggesting that if you have a music studio, art studio, darkroom, shop, or sewing room, you need to shut it down. I am suggesting that, as you contemplate the future, you carefully evaluate the way you are allocating your time *now*. Choose wisely and your decision will reward you. Choose unwisely and your decision may rob you.

YOUR ASSIGNMENT

Here is a short exercise designed to help you evaluate what you need to do with what you have just read. Get a notepad and write these four words in a list on the left side of a blank page:

Physically
Relationally
Professionally
Spiritually

Beside each word write one thing you can begin doing that, if done consistently, would have a positive effect on that component of your life. What small investment in each of those areas can you begin making that you'll be able to look back on as a worthy investment of your time? What can you begin to do consistently—physically, relationally, professionally, and spiritually—that will have cumulative value? What do you wish you had done consistently over the past twelve months in each of those areas? Spending a few minutes answering these questions will provide you with a starting point for using your time more wisely beginning now.

If Job was right, and the number of our days really is determined, if there are limits we cannot exceed, then the issue of how we spend our time is of paramount importance. Indeed, time may be the most crucial arena in which to apply the Best Question Ever. So once again let me ask, in light of your past experience, your current circumstances, and your future hopes and dreams, how should you be allocating your time? What do you need to add to your schedule? What needs to be subtracted? Where do you need to apply the principle of cumulative value?

Your time is your life. What is the wise thing to do?

Part III

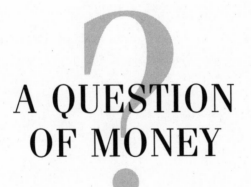

A QUESTION
OF MONEY

10

MONEY WISE

Managing Your Dead Presidents

You already know you would have more money in the bank and greater peace of mind if you had managed your money more wisely. So I won't insult you by trying to convince you of the need for wisdom in this area of your life. And I will not hammer you with statistics. Statistics are what other people have done. Did I mention that consumer debt has tripled since 1980 and that the average American household has over $35,000 in consumer debt? Sorry.

Chances are, if you had been evaluating your financial decisions through the grid of the Best Question Ever, you would live in a slightly smaller house with slightly less expensive furniture. You would be driving a slightly older car. Your television wouldn't be quite as big and your closet wouldn't be quite as full. Basically, you wouldn't be having quite as much fun.

On the positive side of the ledger, your 401(k) would be maxed out, your credit card balance would be zero at the end of the month, and you would feel free to generously support those organizations that are making a positive difference in the world. Maybe I was wrong about the fun.

Believe it or not, if you had been managing your money the way I am about to suggest, you would actually be richer and happier. No, you wouldn't be happier because you were rich. You would be happier because you would be free from the unnecessary pressures that come with poor money management.

The truth is, you are already rich. You have more than you need to live on, and by international standards, you have a surplus of wealth. You can afford to go out to eat, launder your clothes, watch cable or satellite TV, and buy books like this one. You are eating three meals a day and living indoors with cash to spare.

So how does it feel to be wealthy?

You probably have no idea, and here's why.

There's a difference between *being* rich and *feeling* rich. The reason you don't *feel* rich is because you don't actually have any extra cash. It's all spoken for. There's more month than money. There are more bills to pay than bills to pay them. You don't feel rich because you owe more money than you have in your checking account. You don't feel rich because, financially speaking, you are upside down. If suddenly you had to come up with the cash to pay off everyone you owe, including your mortgage lender, you would be out on the street. That's just another way of saying you would be bankrupt.

As long as this is the case you will never feel rich. Instead, you will always feel stressed. Don't miss this: As long as you are upside down financially, it doesn't matter how much money you make—you will never feel rich. Never. The guy who rakes in $350,000 a year but spends $375,000 a year and has twice that much in debt doesn't feel as rich as the woman who makes $50,000 and lives on 75 percent of it with no debt. She's free; he's not. She's wise; he's foolish.

ASKING THE WRONG QUESTIONS

Of all the areas of life that require wisdom, this one should be the easiest to get a handle on. Making decisions about career and relationships and even morality requires us to delve into the intangibles of passion, fear, and God's calling. But money is simple: A certain amount comes in and you tell it what to do. That's pretty much it.

The fact is, in this country, most money problems stem from poor financial management, not low income. How do we know this? Because the two biggest crises Americans face today are obesity and consumer debt. We eat too much and we spend too much. Neither of these problems is caused by earning too little.

But as usual, our propensity is to look for someone else to blame. So overweight people blame McDonald's, while financially overextended people blame the economy or the president or their employers.

The other day I heard a guy ranting and raving on a talk show because his credit card company had hiked up his interest rate. You would have thought they had done something illegal! He was wondering how in the world he could afford to make his minimum payment. I remember thinking, *If I were them, I would have jacked it up, too!* Anybody who's foolish enough to purchase clothing and food on credit is bound to run out of money sooner or later. If I were the credit card company, I would get my money before there's no more money to get. That's why higher-risk customers are charged higher interest rates.

So what's happening? Why is it so easy for us to abandon common sense in the one area where it is easiest to monitor and predict outcomes? Why do we spend so foolishly? Why do we finance things that are immediately worth ten to twenty percent less once we exit the store? Why would we make ourselves slaves to financial institutions who don't even know our names? Why do we intentionally strap on the unnecessary pressure that comes with debt and then complain about it?

Is it greed? Maybe. Is it stupidity? Probably not. Are we all just consumed with keeping up with the people around us? I'm sure that's part of it. But I think there's something else that keeps us on the financial treadmill. We have allowed culture to influence the way we manage money by teaching us to ask all the wrong questions.

Can I afford it?

What will the monthly payment be?

How much can I borrow?

Is it on sale?

How much available equity do I have in my home?

Is it cheaper to lease?

The assumption is that if I *can* make it work financially, I *should* make it work. If I *can* afford it, I *should* afford it. If I *can* borrow it, I *should* borrow it. How easily we forget that nobody in the retail, automobile, or mortgage industry has the least concern about the health of our financial future or the stability of our current financial picture. They are concerned only with our financial history, and they adjust their interest rates accordingly. In other words, the people that we allow to influence our financial decisions are not concerned about how our decisions affect us; they are concerned only with how our decisions affect them. And if you work in any of those industries, you know the trouble and expense your organization has gone to in order to protect the company, not the consumer.

The reason we so easily get upside down financially is because everybody who has anything to sell is working overtime to move us in that direction. The only person looking out for your best interest financially is—you guessed it—*you!* And that means you must ask yourself a *different* set of questions.

The conventional questions are fine for conventional people, but you don't want to be a conventional person, do you? If you look *conventional* up in the thesaurus you will find these synonyms: *standard, normal, typical.*

Think about it. Do you want to be a standard person? How about normal? Typical? Conventional is what everybody else is doing. And you remember what your momma said about that: "If everybody jumped in the fire, would you jump, too?" Financially speaking, if you are like most people, you have already jumped into the fire. And you've gotten burned.

But all of that can change.

COULD VERSUS SHOULD

Conventional financial wisdom is built on the premise that if you can, you should. But when you begin to evaluate your financial decisions through the lens of Best Question Ever, all of that changes. You will stop asking, "What *can* I do?" and ask, "What *should* I do?" Instead of, *"Can* I afford it?" you will ask, *"Should* I afford it." Instead of, *"Can* I lease it?" you will ask, *"Should* I lease it?" Instead of, *"Can* I borrow it?" you will begin asking, *"Should* I borrow it?"

In light of your past financial experience, your current financial picture, and your future financial hopes and dreams, what is the wise thing to do?

Imagine where you would be now if you had been asking and applying that question to all of your financial decisions. The Best Question Ever wrenches control of your financial future out of the hands of those who see you as merely a profit center. The Best Question Ever frees you from the conventional approach to finances—an approach that has robbed most Americans of the freedom that could be theirs if they would simply live on what they make instead of what they can borrow. The Best Question Ever allows you to be content with more of what you have and less of what you want.

A Disturbing Discovery

Asking the right question is one thing; determining the right answer is something else altogether. So before we leave the subject of finances I want to provide you with a specific application. A wise thing to do financially is to reorder the priority you give to your financial categories.

In his book *Master Your Money,* Ron Blue points out that there are really only five things that we do with our money.

1. Spend it.
2. Repay debt.
3. Pay taxes.
4. Save it.
5. Give it.

You may come up with another category or two, but this is where the lion's share of your money goes. Two things govern how much of your money goes toward each of these five categories: priorities and self control. Unfortunately, the order in which I have listed them reflects the majority of people's financial priorities. First we spend. Then we repay debt. We are forced to pay our taxes. If there is any left over we try to save some. And, occasionally, we reach into our wallets and give some away.

Now you may be more intentional about numbers 4 and 5, but if you're like most people, you save and give what's left over. What that means is, you are pilfering from your own future and robbing God's kingdom. Think about it. When saving and giving are your last priorities, you hurt yourself in the future and you withhold from God's kingdom now. Is that the wise thing to do? No, but it is an easy habit to slip into. What would you think of a financial advisor who recommended a strategy like that? Would you hire him as your financial planner? No. You know better. So perhaps it is time to put into practice what you already know to be true.

LEFTOVERS

It's bad enough that we chip away at our family's future financial security by refusing to prioritize saving, but to give God our leftovers is really insulting. My wife, Sandra, is a wonderful cook. Leftovers from Sandra's kitchen are something to look forward to. In spite of that, never once has she prepared a fresh meal for us the night before we were having guests with the intent of serving our guests the leftovers. She wouldn't dream of it. Instead, she honors our guests by serving up the firstfruits of her labor. That's Bible talk for "she pulls out all the stops when we're having company."

If you wouldn't serve your guests leftovers, why would you give God your leftover money? That's like saying, "Sorry, Lord, I wish I could do more, but I can't because I spent most of it on me and gave the rest to Uncle Sam." When we refuse to prioritize giving, it is tantamount to praying, "Heavenly Father, I don't really need Your involvement in my finances. I can handle that arena all by myself. Amen."

On the other hand, giving to kingdom work is an invitation for God to involve Himself in your finances. Throughout the Scriptures, God promises to respond to generous people. Jesus said, "Give, and it will be given to you. A good measure, pressed down, shaken together and running over, will be poured into your lap. For with the measure you use, it will be measured to you" (Luke 6:38, NIV).

To the nation of Israel, God made a similar promise.

"Bring the whole tithe into the storehouse, that there may be food in my house. Test me in this," says the LORD Almighty, "and see if I will not throw open the floodgates of heaven and pour out so much blessing that you will not have room enough for it." (Malachi 3:10, NIV)

God responds to generosity. Giving is an invitation for God to become active in the world of our personal finances. So how does a wise man or woman respond to this insight? They begin to prioritize their giving, and they quit giving God their leftovers. As we will see in the next chapter, when confronted with what God says about generosity, the wise man will reprioritize his entire financial world.

11

UNCONVENTIONAL WISDOM

Reordering Your Financial World

I n what has come to be known as the Sermon on the
Mount, Jesus described how people with perfect faith
would respond to life. We read it and frown. His expectations seem so unrealistic, so impractical. But if you really
believe God is who He says He is and that He will do what
He has promised to do, then Jesus' words make perfect sense.

His words regarding our endless pursuit of *stuff* are par-
ticularly challenging. But if taken to heart they have the
potential to completely reorder your thinking about the pursuit of wealth. I imagine you have read these verses before, but
it won't hurt you to read them again. Don't rush. Allow these
words to sink in.

"Therefore I tell you, do not worry about your life,
what you will eat or drink; or about your body, what

you will wear. Is not life more important than food, and the body more important than clothes? Look at the birds of the air; they do not sow or reap or store away in barns, and yet your heavenly Father feeds them. Are you not much more valuable than they? Who of you by worrying can add a single hour to his life?

"And why do you worry about clothes? See how the lilies of the field grow. They do not labor or spin. Yet I tell you that not even Solomon in all his splendor was dressed like one of these. If that is how God clothes the grass of the field, which is here today and tomorrow is thrown into the fire, will he not much more clothe you, O you of little faith? So do not worry, saying, 'What shall we eat?' or 'What shall we drink?' or 'What shall we wear?' For the pagans run after all these things, and your heavenly Father knows that you need them. But seek first his kingdom and his righteousness, and all these things will be given to you as well." (Matthew 6:25–33, NIV)

Our heavenly Father is not insensitive to our needs and desires. In fact, these verses underscore His commitment to meet our practical earthly needs. The problem, according to Jesus, is not that we need certain things; the problem is the priority we place on meeting those needs. Our concern becomes worry. Our worry reflects a lack of faith. Our lack of faith surfaces in our priorities. So we prioritize our wants and wishes first and God's kingdom last.

Jesus suggests that we reverse the order.

"Seek ye first."

In contrast to putting God's kingdom last, He exhorts us to put it first. And then He makes a promise: "and all these things will be given to you as well." "All these things" is the stuff of life that we pursue to the neglect of God's kingdom. "All these things" is what we eat, where we live, what we wear. It is the stuff that consumes the majority of our financial resources.

Essentially, Jesus is offering us a deal. He will take responsibility for our needs if we will prioritize His kingdom. If we will transfer our concern to what's important to Him, He will take responsibility for what is important to us. This is why I say with confidence that seeking Him first with our money is an invitation for His intervention and involvement in that arena of our lives.

THE FLIP

If you take His promise seriously, what is the wise thing to do as it relates to your finances? I would suggest that you flip the list we discussed in the previous chapter. Remember, we said there are basically five things we do with our money. The new, reprioritized list looks like this:

1. Give it.
2. Save it.

3. Pay taxes.
4. Repay debt.
5. Spend it.

Give First

If giving to kingdom work invites God into your finances, then the first check you ought to write after you get paid is a check to support His kingdom. This is how you "seek first" with your money. When you give first it is the equivalent of saying, "Father, I want to make sure Your kingdom is fully funded. I'll live on the leftovers."

Give before you spend. How much? The New Testament doesn't give us a percentage. But I can't imagine giving anything less than a tithe—that is, 10 percent. It's a small price to pay to get God in the mix. Besides, it is all His anyway. If you don't have enough faith to begin with a tithe, then pick a lower percentage. But make sure you choose a percentage. Percentage giving is the way to begin.

I'm often asked by people who have mismanaged their money if they should wait to begin giving after they have paid off all their creditors. My answer is always the same: "Do you want God to help you now or after you've paid off all your debt?" Remember, generosity is an invitation. I've seen dozens of cases where people were able to get their financial house in order much quicker than they imagined when they committed to percentage, off-the-top giving.

Pay Yourself Second

What's the wise thing to do once you have funded God's kingdom? Fund your own. The next check you need to write is a check to yourself. Specifically, you need to put some money in savings. Again, pick a percentage. Even if it is just two or three percent. Pay yourself second. When you put money in savings, you take it out of circulation. Circulating, easy-to-get-to money quickly evaporates. That's why you rarely have any money left over to save at the end of the month. So what is the wise thing to do? Fund your future at the beginning of the month.

Retire Debt

Next, you need to retire debt. Most consumer debt is dumb debt. You know that. We all have some dumb debt in our past. Dumb debt is debt on items that aren't worth the price you paid once you walked out of the store and drove away. When the interest you pay on an item translates into your having paid ten or twenty percent more than the original price, that's some seriously dumb debt. Once you adopt the Best Question Ever you will find it increasingly difficult to accrue dumb debt.

But what about your current debt? I would suggest you go on a mission. Borrowing a line from Dave Ramsey, you need to dump your debt. Consumer interest eats up your cash flow—cash that you could give, save, or spend. Come up with a plan and set a date for eliminating all but your mortgage debt. If you don't have a deadline, you will never cross the finish line. The deadline will motivate you. It will be a light at the end of your financial tunnel. If necessary, get some help. As we will discuss later on, wise people surround themselves with wise counsel. Asking for help is not a sign of weakness; it is evidence of wisdom.

Pay Your Taxes

Taxes are a fact of life. But if you give generously and save wisely, you will pay less in taxes.

Spend

Finally, we get to the item that generally tops our list. Once you have given, saved, paid down debt, and funded your state, national, and local governments, you get to go shopping!

"With what?" you ask.

With the leftovers.

Now before you decide to line your birdcage with pages from this book, I want you to think about something: What if you had been prioritizing this way for the past five years? Think about how much money you would have saved. Think of the extra cash you would have had if you weren't constantly juggling credit card bills. This isn't the *easy* thing to do, but I would argue that it is the *wise* thing to do.

In light of your past experience, your current circumstances, and your future hopes and dreams, isn't it time to reprioritize your finances?

Try it for three months. Just three months. Write your first check to kingdom work. Your second check to savings. Pay down debt. If money is taken out of your check to cover your taxes, then live on the rest. At the end of three months, evaluate the results. I believe you will discover that God is true to His promise. If you seek first His kingdom, if you walk wisely, then all the other things we have a tendency to worry about will be taken care of.

Part IV

A QUESTION
OF MORALITY

12

SEX FOR DUMMIES

Why Aren't These People Smiling?

The simple message of these next few chapters is one I have spent fifteen years of my life trying to instill in the minds and hearts of American teenagers. Some listened and applied. Through the years I have received countless letters and e-mails from students thanking me for this uncomplicated yet profound principle. Many of these former students are married now and enjoying the rewards of having chosen the path of wisdom in this area of life.

Unfortunately, many more chose not to heed my warnings. And that's understandable. Every day, students are bombarded with messages and images that support a different viewpoint—a view fueled by the God-given passions raging inside their overstimulated and underdisciplined bodies. Besides, I'm old enough to be their dad. What could *I* possibly know?

Nothing has stolen more dreams, dashed more hopes,

broken up more families, and messed up more people psychologically than our propensity to disregard God's commands regarding sexual purity. Most of the major social ills in America are caused by, or fueled by, the misuse of our sexuality. If issues related to sexual impurity—adultery, the shrapnel associated with adultery, addiction to pornography, AIDS and other sexually transmitted diseases, abortion, the psychological effects associated with abortion, sexual abuse, incest, rape, and all sexual addictions—were to suddenly disappear from society, imagine the resources we would have available to apply to the handful of issues that would remain.

Since God grants us free will, there will always be people who will themselves into the complications associated with sexual impurity. This, too, is a fact of life. But for the sake of those who are willing to listen, the warning must be sounded.

SLOW LEARNERS

I started this book by saying that we have all done things we regret. We regret some decisions because they are embarrassing. Other regrets stem from decisions that ate up our time or wasted our resources. But no regret runs deeper than the regret associated with unwise moral decisions. In time you may find you are able to laugh about wasted money and poor time management. But when it comes to moral failure, time doesn't help. Nobody ever laughs about an affair, a divorce, a sexual addiction, or abuse. In the arena of moral failure, the regret runs deep and the pain can traverse generations. Chances are, your greatest regrets in life fall somewhere within this category.

The strange thing is, as predictable as the outcomes are, we don't appear to have learned very much. One would think that after losing thousands of people to sexually transmitted diseases and watching a generation or two of kids grow up without fathers in their homes, we might have learned something. But alas, lust and greed continue to drive us past the limits afforded by common sense.

I was reminded of how predictable certain outcomes are one afternoon while sitting in my chiropractor's waiting room. I struck up a conversation with a woman whose son was reading a book I had read, and she asked me if I was a teacher. When I informed her that I was a pastor, she launched into a detailed account of her unfaithful husband and subsequent divorce. When she mentioned that her husband had run off with his younger secretary, I responded, "Now that was original." Not dissuaded by my sarcasm, she went on to talk about how quickly he had married his mistress and how difficult it was to find a job that left her with the flexibility she needed to raise their middle-school-aged son.

I shook my head and said, "Well, let me assure you of one thing: Your husband is far more miserable than you will ever be."

She looked confused, as did the other people in the

waiting room who were pretending not to listen to what was quickly becoming a potential script idea for *The Sopranos*.

"What do you mean by that?" she asked.

"Well, pretty soon your ex's new wife is going to want to start a family. He's not going to want to do that because he already did that once. She's going to be upset, and either way he goes, he's not going to get what he wants. One day he's going to wake up and realize that he is stuck."

Immediately, the guy to my left, whose nose had been buried in his newspaper, blurted out, "You got that right!" Apparently I had hit a nerve. But since I had already opened up one can of worms, I just ignored his comment and focused on my new friend.

She sat up a little straighter and actually smiled at the thought of her ex suffering for a change. "You know, I didn't think about that. But I bet you're right. And he's definitely not going to want to start another family."

Now she was starting to sound a little *too* giddy. Then she turned and said, "But how did you know all of that?"

"I'm a pastor," I said. "I've seen this played out more times than I can count. Solomon was right: There's nothing new under the sun."

She shook her head. "Yeah, I guess you are right. But when you're in the middle of it, you think you are the only one."

And there you have it.

When you're in the middle of it, you think you are the only one.

WHEN THE FOG ROLLS IN

Do you know why people are prone to make such foolish moral decisions? Because something always whispers to us that our situation is unique: *Nobody has ever felt this way before. No one has had to deal with what I have to deal with. I can handle it. I'm not like everybody else. The statistics don't apply to me. The statistics don't apply to my kids. I know what's best for me. My passion runs deep; love will keep us alive.*

As long as you are convinced that your situation and feelings are unique, you will resist the Best Question Ever. Now, that might seem to contradict the entire premise of the question—after all, your uniqueness is what makes this question so powerful. But in this context we are not talking about your individuality as it relates to your past, your present, and your future dreams. In that way, you *are* unique.

But there is nothing unique about your circumstances, your emotions, your desires, and your passions. And as long as you deceive yourself into thinking that you are the first to feel what you are feeling, you will chase those feelings to the neglect of wisdom. And at the end of the day you will discover that you are not so unique after all. The outcomes are predictable. Lonely is lonely, no matter how much money you make. Addicted is addicted, no matter who you know. Guilty is guilty, no matter what you drive. Depressed is depressed, no matter what you take.

IT CUTS BOTH WAYS

Now here's some good news. In fact, here is the reason the Best Question Ever is such a powerful ally in avoiding sexual sin, with all its complications and consequences: While the outcomes of sexual sin are predictable, the decisions that set us up to sin sexually are equally predictable. And—and this is a big *and*—the Best Question Ever will enable you to see those decisions for what they really are. If you are willing to face up to the fact that your temptation, circumstances, and feelings are not unique to you, the Best Question Ever will empower you to make choices that will set you up for success rather than failure in this crucial arena of life.

Again, the outcomes of certain behaviors are predictable, as are the steps leading to those behaviors. The sooner we face up to that humbling reality, the sooner we will quit trusting our hearts and choose to ask the Best Question Ever—a question provided by our heavenly Father for those who want to look back with gratitude rather than regret.

Up until this point, you may feel like I've been circling the runway. So please put away your tray tables and return your seat to its upright and locked position. And be forewarned, the next few minutes may be a little bumpy.

13

HINDSIGHT

The Saga of Frank and Sheila

Think for a moment about your greatest moral regret.
That night, that embrace, that purchase, that long
glance, walking through that door…

I told you this might be a bit bumpy.

I know, it is probably something you work hard not to
think about. You may have promised yourself you would
never think about it again. And that may have been a good
idea. But now that I've dredged it up, hold on to it for just
a moment. There may even be a whole list for you to choose
from. And they may not be in the distant past. Whatever the
case, play along and pick one.

Now I want you to think back to the decisions preceding
the event or relationship you regret most. At some point you
have probably rehearsed some of these decisions in your mind.

I wish I had never taken that job.

I wish I had never called her.

I wish I had never accepted his invitation.

I wish I had never taken that trip.

I wish I had never subscribed to____.

I wish I had listened to my mama.

If you think back far enough you can probably string together a series of decisions that led you to the brink of the moment or season you now regret.

My point?

Our greatest moral regrets are always preceded by a series of *unwise* choices. Not wrong choices, not impermissible, not illegal, but unwise. We *choose* ourselves to the brink of disaster because none of the choices we make along the way are "wrong." So we don't hesitate. Then we defend our actions with the anemic excuse, "I couldn't help myself," followed by the equally ridiculous question, "How did I get into this mess?"

A more helpful and honest question to ask is, "How did I get *myself* into this mess?" The answer to that question is the same for everybody. *Everybody.* Once we follow our passions, there ain't nothing new under the sun.

How did we get ourselves into such a mess? We made a series of unwise choices. Unwise choices that sent us beyond the point of no return. The names and faces change, but the sequences and outcomes are tragically similar. We may think our situation is different and, therefore, what is wise for most isn't wise for us. But in the end…well, I think we've covered that sufficiently.

You know what's so ironic? When someone we know

begins inching toward moral disaster, we can see it so clearly. Take Frank and Sheila, for example.

OFFICE PARTY

Sheila and Frank work in the same office. Frank is married. Sheila's single. Sheila is attractive. Frank notices, but he's a committed husband and father—he made a vow and he plans to keep it.

One day while they're working together on a team project, Frank thinks, *Hey, I could ask Sheila to go to lunch. It's professional—we'll talk about work stuff.* He feels a slight twinge of hesitation, but he tells himself, *There's nothing wrong with eating lunch with a work associate. We've got to eat lunch. Besides, we'll be in a public restaurant.* So he shoots her an e-mail inviting her to lunch.

Sheila reads the e-mail and thinks it a bit odd that Frank would ask her to lunch. *He's married, for one thing,* she thinks. *I don't know what we will talk about for an hour. But what can it hurt? Besides, he is pretty influential around here, and there's certainly nothing wrong with having lunch with a coworker.*

So she accepts.

So far, nobody has done anything wrong or even out of the ordinary. But let's be honest. How wise is it for a married man to go to lunch with a single female coworker whom he finds attractive? In light of his future hopes and dreams for himself and his family, is there any upside to this? And from

Sheila's perspective, what can be gained from lunch with Frank? The risk far outweighs the rewards.

A few weeks later the team is working late, and when dinnertime rolls around Frank's thoughts turn to Sheila. She was easy to talk to and a lot more sophisticated than the guys in the group. Their profanity and stories of business-trip exploits always got on his nerves. He wouldn't have to endure all of that with Sheila. Again, there is a twinge of hesitation, but he sweeps it aside. *Everybody's got to eat dinner,* he thinks. *There is nothing wrong with having dinner with a friend.*

Sheila is flattered and hungry. Frank was easy to talk to, and since he is married, she knows she doesn't have to worry about him hitting on her like the less-than-subtle single guys in the group.

Do I even need to finish this? It is so typical. So predictable. And yet, up until this point, nobody has done anything wrong, illegal, or immoral. What Frank and Sheila (and their real-life counterparts) don't realize is that these are not individual, unrelated decisions they are making. They are on a path. They are moving in a direction. A direction that is obvious to everybody but them. And if you were to drop into their imaginary world and question them about their relationship, they would respond like all of us have responded at one time or another when confronted about the path we trod: "I'm not doing anything wrong!" And that is deceptively true.

LATER THAT NIGHT...

During dinner, Sheila asks Frank about his family. *That ought to establish some safe boundaries*, she thinks. Unfortunately, things aren't going too well with Frank's marriage. When he tried to share his woes with his friend Denny the week before, Denny just shrugged his shoulders and changed the subject. But Sheila listens. She even asks questions. What's more, she offers Frank some good advice. *If only my wife thought more like this*, he muses.

Now what Frank and Sheila don't realize is that their relationship just moved to a new level. They have, unbeknownst to either of them, slipped across the border into the outskirts of intimacy. Have they been intimate? Nope. Nobody has touched anybody. If Frank's wife were to walk in, he could introduce her to Sheila with a clear conscience. But this conversation is the beginning of a different kind of relationship. And relationships almost always pick up where they left off.

As their team draws closer to their deadline, Frank's boss suggests that he split the team into three smaller groups so they can work on three components simultaneously. As Frank gazes at the list of people on the team, he has a decision to make. Should he pair himself up with Shelia?

If this were a movie, this would be the part where you would want to stand up in the theater and shout, "Don't do it! Run! Go home! Get another job! Think about your kids!"

I wonder if God ever shouts those kinds of warnings at us? In the Old Testament that was the role of the prophet. They usually ended up in jail, and the people they were shouting at usually ended up in trouble.

So here's Frank, staring at his list. In his mind, this is a small decision. Looking back, this would be the decision he would regret most. Looking in the rearview mirror, this would be the day he would wish he could relive. This would be the decision he would most like to take back.

He hesitates. Once again, something tells Frank not to do it. But hey, there's nothing *wrong* with working together on a project, right? The fact is, they have already been working together and this isn't anything new. There is no logical reason *not* to. In fact, there are a half-dozen good reasons to do it. So he writes her name next to his.

Okay, let's get this over with.

One night Frank offers to drive Sheila home from work. She invites him in. When Frank crosses her threshold, their relationship moves deeper into the realm of intimacy. This time they feel it. There is nothing professional about any of this; this is all personal. But nothing happened. Nothing "wrong" or even "inappropriate." They chat for few minutes and Frank leaves. But at this point you can stick a fork in it.

The next morning Darla asks Frank where he had been so late. And even though there was nothing *wrong* with stopping at Sheila's house, Frank doesn't feel it's necessary to mention it. Again, nobody has done anything wrong. Nothing has happened. But if Frank were to share it with Darla, you can bet your car *she* would think something was wrong.

Why? Because Darla is smart enough to know that relationships don't stand still. They are always going somewhere. She wouldn't respond to what had "happened." She would react to where the whole thing was "headed." That's how wise people (and suspicious spouses) think.

Two nights later the same situation occurs, but this time Frank embraces Sheila at the door. They both know it is wrong. But the wheels of rationalization have been churning for so long that their excuses overwhelm their collective consciences. And you know the rest of the story—a story with a disturbing moral.

14

LIFE RULES

Living Far from the Edge

T he adventures of Frank and Sheila underscore an extraordinary, life-changing, future-altering principle: *Every poor moral decision is prefaced by a series of unwise choices.*

The irresistible urge that neither Frank nor Sheila had the willpower to overcome that night on the front porch was the culmination of a series of unwise choices. The feelings they misinterpreted as love, fate, destiny, and all the other silly things that drive people would have been nonexistent if they had chosen the path of wisdom. Theirs was a series of unwise choices that set them up for the one decision that would send their lives tumbling in a new and unenviable direction.

Imagine if either or both had paused early on in their relationship to ask the $19.95 question: *What is the wise thing to do?*

What if Frank or Sheila had been willing to face up to what was at stake rather than focus on where the line was between right and wrong? They had several opportunities to change the outcome of the story if either of them had been willing to ask and apply the Best Question Ever.

Every poor moral decision is prefaced by a series of unwise choices.

Got it?

Think once again about your greatest moral regret. Isn't it true that your decision to cross a certain moral line was predicated by a series of choices that led to that final and most regretful one? And isn't it true that you marched right along, justifying every choice with, *There's nothing wrong with...*

And you were right. There probably was nothing wrong with most of those preliminary choices. But looking back, it's all too clear, isn't it? One "nothing wrong with" choice led to another, until the temptation was irresistible.

LIFE ON THE EDGE

So many things in our culture bait us to the edge of moral disaster. And because it is all legal, acceptable, and permissible, we take the bait. We read the magazines, pipe in the movies, stare at the pictures, laugh at the jokes, wear the clothes, and listen to the music.

Let's face it, purity is not a cultural value. Neither is modesty. While adultery is still frowned upon in most quarters, the impropriety that leads to adultery is actually encouraged, even celebrated. Similarly, teenage pregnancy is still considered a social evil. But again, the activities, fashion, and music that drive adolescents in that direction are not generally frowned upon. Parents fund the very activities that create the context for the act they consider so abhorrent. As long as we take our cues from the culture, purity and modesty will always be in the rearview mirror. Those lines will be crossed without a second thought. And once those lines are crossed, sexual misconduct is one easy decision away.

I was reminded of all this a few years ago when I was asked to participate in a task force designed to fight pornography. After about an hour of discussion, I raised my hand and asked what to me was an obvious question: "What exactly are we fighting? What *is* pornography?"

I won't pollute your mind or these pages with the definition I was given. Suffice it to say, the stuff I'm confronted with daily that I'm committed to not putting in my mind, the stuff I'm trying to protect my kids from—these didn't even register with this group. What they were fighting was so far past the line of what I consider decent that I quit the task force. I remember thinking, *If that's the line of decency and acceptability, this war has already been lost.*

My point? Each of us, at a personal level, must scramble back to some long-abandoned standard of purity and modesty. If we don't, we will always find ourselves on the brink of moral disaster. Culture has drawn the line of decency far too close to the edge. To accept the standard handed to us by our culture is to live and relate in a very dangerous place.

The Best Question Ever, however, will lead you to a place of safety, a place where there is margin for error. Let me illustrate.

POLITICALLY INCORRECT

I decided at the beginning of our marriage not to eat alone with or ride in a car alone with another woman other than members of my family. I made this decision based upon the experience of countless others who readily admitted that their extramarital relationships began with something as innocent as a meal or a business trip. I figured that by eliminating those two activities I would be eliminating two possible contexts for temptation. Later I added a third component to my personal commandments: I decided not to counsel alone with women.

Whenever I share these decisions publicly, I watch men and women shake their heads in disbelief. For most people it sounds impractical, even insensitive. And I would never suggest that everybody adopt my standards. And I would be quick to acknowledge that there is nothing "wrong" with any of the behaviors I have mentioned. But I would also be quick to point out that neither Sandra nor I have ever regretted my decision, even though it has caused some awkward situations with people who didn't understand and who took it personally. Through the years I have met scores of people who wish they had adopted similar standards earlier in their careers.

Why go to such impractical lengths? Because every regretful moral decision is preceded by a series of unwise choices—unwise choices that don't raise an eyebrow or infringe upon our culturally programmed consciences. Everybody has certain lines they never intend to cross. But why draw those lines so close to the edge? Why set standards where the tug to ignore those standards is seemingly irresistible?

Men, let me ask you a really stupid question. What's more difficult, resisting the temptation to ask someone to lunch or resisting the temptation to embrace an attractive woman who has invited you into her home? Remember the "I couldn't help myself" excuse I derided in the previous chapter? Can you understand why this is such an anemic excuse for anything? Of course we can't "help ourselves" in certain situations. We have led ourselves to the brink of disaster.

Ladies, what is more difficult, saying no to an invitation to lunch or resisting the advances of a man you are infatuated with, a man whom you have invited into your home late at night after a couple of drinks? "But I would never let things go that far," you argue. Of course you wouldn't. In fact, everybody who has ever allowed things to go that far never intended for them to go that far. That's exactly why things went that far. Men and women didn't *intend* for them to, so consequently, they trusted their intentions to keep them out of trouble.

Wake up! You never *intended* to get yourself into *any* of the situations you now regret. Right? Your financial, moral, professional, and relational regrets all came about unintentionally. Nobody intends to blow up a marriage. Nobody intends to bury themselves in debt. Nobody intends to destroy a career. Nobody intends to alienate themselves from their children. Nobody intends to become addicted to anything. Your own experience substantiates the fact that intentions are pretty much a worthless defense against temptation and regret. It takes more than good intentions to cross the finish line in any area of life.

None of us plan—or intend—to get into trouble. The problem is, we don't plan *not* to. Adopting the Best Question Ever enables us to plan not to. The Best Question Ever puts feet to our intentions. It gives us traction to stand our ground against the seemingly overwhelming current of culture.

Here's how it works.

15

EXTREME MEASURES

Playing It Safe

The Best Question Ever will lead you away from the brink of a decision you may regret to a place of safety. This fact alone is why it is so easy to disregard the Best Question Ever in the arena of sexuality. Like you, I don't want to miss out on anything life has to offer. So my natural inclination is to ask, "Where's the line between right and wrong?" Once that is established, I want to cozy up to the line and live right there. To do otherwise may mean missing out on something good.

At the same time, I don't want to do anything now that will haunt me in the future. And there's a part of me that wants to please my heavenly Father. So once I've recognized where the line is, I try not to cross it. The problem with this approach is that there is no margin for error. In most areas of life that is not a problem. If the speed limit is fifty-five miles per hour, I drive fifty-five miles per hour. If my thoughts drift and I find myself roaring down the highway at sixty miles per hour, no harm done. I just ease off the gas. When I was sixteen and my curfew was midnight, I tried to time it so that I arrived home right at midnight. I gave myself no margin for error. If I was a few minutes late, no problem, no consequences. If you violate the guidelines of your diet for a day, no problem. You just ease back into your routine the following day.

But when you cross certain lines sexually, there are always consequences, sometimes for the rest of your life. Slipping over "the line" in this particular arena of life can mean kids growing up without a dad in the home. It can result in women fending for themselves financially while trying to raise their children. It means men living with the constant distraction of images they can't erase from their minds. It means young ladies losing the opportunity to give themselves wholly to their husbands on their wedding night. It means men constantly struggling not to compare their wives to other women they have slept with in the past. It can mean living with the burden of an incurable disease. As in the case of three friends of mine, crossing certain lines sexually can mean death—death that leaves a hole in a family, a mother mourning the loss of a child, brothers and sisters devastated. In the case of the HIV epidemic in Africa, crossing certain lines morally has resulted in hundreds of thousands of homeless children.

Let me be blunt. To leave yourself no margin for error

morally is about the most insensitive thing you can do to those you love. Relationally, it is a death wish. It is the worst kind of arrogance. It is tantamount to a recovering alcoholic walking into a bar and sitting down on a bar stool, all the while justifying his actions with the excuse, "There's nothing wrong with being here as long as I'm not drinking."

STEPPING BACK

Wisdom would dictate that we establish some artificial boundaries a safe distance away from the moral point of no return. Boundaries so far from the brink of disaster that, should you violate one, the consequences would be minimal. Thus, my decision not to be alone with women in certain environments.

I hesitate to include this next example lest you think I'm a total societal reject. But you're more than halfway through the book now, so you might as well finish. And let me qualify this by saying that I'm not suggesting anybody follow my lead on this. It's just an example of something I did based on what I thought was wise for me.

I didn't own a television until I was thirty.

Am I a freak or what?

I lived alone during graduate school, and I knew what a subscription to cable would pipe into my apartment. I didn't want to deal with the temptation, so I never purchased a TV. After graduate school I bought a nice condo in Atlanta. My parents gave me a beautiful cherrywood television cabinet. But I didn't purchase a television until four years later when I married Sandra.

I can't begin to tell you how many people kept trying to give me a television. They would open up my cabinet and ask, "Where's the TV?"

"I don't have one."

"You don't *have* one?"

"No."

"We've got an extra one you can have."

No one understood and I wasn't about to explain. But I knew from experience that it was easier to resist the temptation to buy a television than it was to control what I watched.

Do you think I now regret that decision? Do you suppose I look back on those ten years and think how much richer my life would be if only I'd had a television all that time? Not for a second. Would it have been *wrong* for me to own a television? Nope. But knowing what I knew then, I felt it would be unwise. Knowing what I know now, I think it was one of the best decisions I ever made.

Extreme? Yes. But in light of the extreme consequences of a moral failure, isn't extreme precaution appropriate? Let's turn it around and look at it through a different set of lenses.

How extreme do you want your current or future spouse to be when it comes to protecting himself or herself from unnecessary temptation in this arena? You may want to close the book and think about that for a few minutes.

Your answer to this question will help you cut through the fog of self-deception. After all, what's appropriate for your spouse is certainly appropriate for you.

Try this. To what extreme would you be willing to go to protect your children from having to navigate the complexities of a home divided over someone's sexual impropriety, be it adultery or a sexual addiction? What precautions would you be willing to take in order to ensure that they never have to suffer through the emotional complications of a broken home?

In light of what is at stake, what is the wise thing for you to do? In light of what you want for your marriage and your family, what is the wise thing to do? In light of the extreme consequences associated with moral failure, what extreme measures are you willing to take? To what extreme are you willing to go to protect what's most important to you?

BUT WHAT ABOUT...

Yes, people will chuckle, and your close friends may not understand. Yes, it will complicate things at times, and it will not always be convenient. And yes, it will send an unspoken message to your family about how important they are to you. No, you will never regret it.

Having waded with broken people through just about every scenario imaginable, I thought it might be helpful, if not meddlesome, to share the top five environments in which the seeds for moral failure are sown in the life of a married person. And let me go ahead and state up front, there's nothing *wrong* with any of these things:

- Chatting on-line with members of the opposite sex

- Dinner after work with members of the opposite sex

- Working with a personal trainer of the opposite sex

- Counseling with members of the opposite sex

- Ladies' night out dancing while husbands stay home

I've seen so much heartbreak stemming from these five situations that it is easy for me to eliminate these as options for my life. Especially number five. I never get invited.

Wisdom dictates that each of us set standards that keep us out of harm's way. These should be boundaries that are so far from the line of regret that, were we to cross one, we would suffer little or no consequence. When these are in place, a fascinating dynamic occurs: Your conscience actually latches on to the artificial standard you have set. When you violate one of your self-imposed rules, you feel guilty. And that low-risk guilt serves as a reminder that you are venturing out into dangerous territory.

CONSCIENCE POINT

Some time ago I traveled to Dallas with Sandra to speak at a leadership conference. I'd been asked to come a day early to visit several radio and TV stations and do interviews to promote the event. I was informed that a driver would pick me up at the hotel at 8:00 AM and escort me back and forth between stations. I assumed the driver would be a man. Never assume anything. Sandra, meanwhile, decided to spend that day shopping with a friend.

That morning I stepped outside the hotel at the appointed time to meet my ride. Parked in front of the hotel was a nice white Lexus with a woman sitting alone in the driver's seat. I thought to myself, *There's a nice white Lexus with a woman sitting in the driver's seat. I wonder where my ride is?*

While I stood waiting, the woman finally stepped out of the car and said, "Are you Andy Stanley?"

I said yes.

"I'm your escort," she said.

Suddenly I felt very uncomfortable. Why? Was it because it is a sin for me to be alone in a car with a woman? Nope. That wasn't it at all. I was uncomfortable because my conscience had become attuned to the standard I had set for myself. And she could tell I was hesitating to get in the car.

I didn't want to make things awkward for her, so I got in the car and we drove to our first appointment. And it felt really weird. As soon as I got the chance, I called Sandra and told her what had transpired. I sounded so stressed on the phone that she laughed. To make matters worse, the lady kept introducing herself to people as my escort. I, on the other hand, felt the urge to tell everybody we met that I didn't usually ride around alone with women. The truth be known, nobody really cared about any of that but me; nobody gave it a second thought. But I felt uncomfortable the entire day. And I'm glad I did.

Wherever the Best Question Ever leads you to set boundaries for your behavior, your conscience will take up residency there as well.

Perhaps you've begun to wonder if I'm overreacting just a bit, that maybe I'm taking this whole thing a little too seriously. And perhaps you are right. Maybe I am over-reacting. But having talked to so many people who have underreacted and paid dearly, I would rather err on the side of caution. And for the record, as I read the Scriptures, it appears our heavenly Father would have us err on the side of caution as well.

16

FLEE!

The Wisdom of Flight

In Paul's letter to Christians living in the city of Corinth, a city known for its tolerance of sexual impropriety, he penned these words:

Regarding sexual immorality, pursue all manner of sensuality and impurity, yet remain faithful to God and your spouse. Husbands, gaze upon women in a lustful fashion until your heart is full, but do not touch that which is forbidden. Wives, dress in a manner that provokes the lustful passions of the men around you, but in your actions remain faithful to your husband.

That's from 3 Corinthians, the lost epistle.

Just kidding. Go ahead and look—it's not in there. But doesn't that pretty much describe our approach?

Actually, what Paul had to say was far more succinct: "Flee from sexual immorality" (1 Corinthians 6:18, NIV).

The Greek term translated *flee* means "flee." As in, "run really fast in the opposite direction." No doubt you have fled from something in your lifetime—an oncoming car, your neighbor's dog, a linebacker, your big sister. We all know what it means to flee.

When I was in third grade, I shot my sister with a toy arrow. My dad took the arrow and began chasing me through the house. I fled. I ran into the bathroom and sat down on the toilet to keep him from spanking me with the arrow. Unfortunately, the lid was open and I fell in wearing my favorite footy pajamas. My dad laughed so hard that he couldn't spank me.

When I was in fifth grade, I was walking with a buddy across a pasture when we looked up and saw a herd of cattle stampeding in our direction. We fled. When we reached the barbed-wire fence, we dove underneath and rolled to safety.

There is a certain emotion associated with fleeing. Fear. We flee when we know we are in danger. Fear prompts us to flee. The reason we don't flee sexual immorality is that we don't fear it; we naively believe we can handle it. So instead of fleeing, we flirt with it. We snuggle up next to it. We dance around the edges. After all, we aren't doing anything *wrong*.

There's nothing wrong with standing out in the middle of an open pasture with a herd of stampeding cattle heading your way, either. There's not one verse of Scripture that prohibits such behavior. I have never heard a sermon on the subject. In fact the United States Constitution protects your right to do so. But nonetheless, it is a stupid thing to do. And by the time you've learned your lesson, you won't have another opportunity to apply what you've learned.

IN A CATEGORY ALL ITS OWN

Paul doesn't stop with his four-word warning. He goes on to make one of the most profound statements in the New Testament: "All other sins a man commits are outside his body, but he who sins sexually sins against his own body."

Sexual sin is in a category all its own. It is the most dangerous kind of sin. Anyone who has done any significant amount of counseling knows this to be the case. Sexual sin wreaks havoc with the soul, whether male or female. The shame runs deep and the regret runs wide, often seeping into every facet of a person's life. Long after men and women come to grips with God's forgiveness, those who have sinned sexually still wrestle to forgive *themselves*. I don't know why I bother to write this in the third person. We all know this to be true from personal experience, either our own or that of someone close to us.

So flee! Don't hesitate. Don't look back. Don't try to endure it. Don't flirt with it. Don't fool yourself. Don't try to be strong. Run! Like a coiled snake, sexual temptation has a considerable striking distance. You are never as safe as you think.

FLEEING 101

In light of your past experience, current circumstances, and future hopes and dreams, what is the wise thing for you to do in order to avoid regret in this area of life?

If your past is dotted with moral failure, then it would be wise to establish extraordinarily conservative boundaries. Your past points to the fact that you are more susceptible in this area than the average person; consequently, you can't be content with average boundaries.

Through the years, I have had numerous conversations with young men who have been very sexually active before coming to faith in Christ. From their past experience, dating was almost synonymous with sex—sex was pretty much the goal of a date. Coming to faith in Christ didn't automatically erase those leanings.

My advice to a young man or woman coming from that kind of past is always the same: Don't date for a year. I tell them to get out their calendars, look ahead one year, and circle the date. They always stare at me with the same look of disbelief. Some listen, some don't. Those who do come back and thank me. Those who don't, don't.

Why a year? Isn't that a bit extreme? Yep. But those who've taken the challenge will tell you that what God did in their hearts during that year prepared them to venture back into the world of romance with a completely different perspective on relationships. Many of these young men and women are happily married now. They consider their decision not to date to be a defining moment in their lives.

I know young ladies who went out and found female roommates in order to have some built-in accountability. I know of young adults who moved back home in order to avoid unnecessary temptation. I know young men who have canceled their Internet service. These are people who, because of their past, took extreme measures in response to the Best Question Ever. And while their friends chuckled, they were set free.

You Must Decide

As we said earlier, the Best Question Ever enables us to plan *not* to get into trouble. Asking the question enables us to stand our ground against the seemingly overwhelming current of culture. Applied to the arena of sexual purity, the Best Question Ever enables us to make a clean break with the past and move purposely toward our hopes and dreams.

But to leverage this powerful principle you will need to predecide some things. You need to predecide about what are and are not appropriate environments. If you are single, you need to predecide how physically involved you should become in a dating context. You need to predecide your entertainment options.

All of this might strike you as a bit overboard. Extreme. Maybe even legalistic. But here's what I know. When men

and women and teenagers are confronted with the consequences of their moral impropriety they all say the same
thing: "I would give anything—*anything*—to be able to go
back and undo what I've done."

Anything? Isn't that a bit extreme? They don't think so.
Perhaps you, too, would be willing to go to extreme measures if it meant being able to undo certain moments of your
life. So why not take extreme precautions up front instead
of facing the reality that even extreme sacrifices on the back
end won't erase the past?

If you don't decide some of these things ahead of time,
somebody else will decide for you. If you don't have your own
personal standards, somebody else will force theirs on you.
Everyone agrees that there are lines that shouldn't be crossed.
You must conduct your relationships within the boundaries
you have set for yourself in light of your past experience, your
current circumstances, and your future hopes and dreams.

Had you adopted the Best Question Ever earlier in your
life, perhaps your greatest regrets could have been avoided. If
you adopt it now, future regrets can be avoided. The Best
Question Ever enables you to experience what God originally
intended when He gave mankind the precious gift of sexuality.

A DESIGNER GIFT

In the beginning God didn't just create the heavens and the
earth. In the beginning God created sex. It was His idea! Is

God good, or what? Better yet, after creating it, He gave it to us as a gift! I know you've thanked God for a lot of things, but have you ever thanked Him for the gift of sex?

He gave sex to us as a gift—a gift that comes with instructions. Contrary to popular opinion, the guidelines for using this Designer gift were created to enhance our experience, not diminish it. God is not against sex. He's all for it! The parameters He has set are evidence that He is for *you* as well. For within these boundaries a man and a woman are able to experience something that goes way beyond physical satisfaction. When sex is enjoyed the way God originally intended, the result is *intimacy*. When we ignore God's guidelines, we pay the price in the very realm sex was designed to enhance—intimacy.

So once again we find ourselves asking this confining yet liberating question: What is the wise thing to do?

In light of my past experience, what is the wise thing to do going forward? In light of what's going on in my life right now—the health of my marriage or the nature of my current dating relationships—what is the wise thing to do? And as I contemplate the future—the legacy I want to leave for my kids, the prospect of finishing strong in my marriage, the story I want to tell my future spouse—what is the wise thing to do?

No, it won't always be easy to do the wise thing. But you've already experienced enough of life to know that it will be worth it.

Part V

WISDOM FOR
THE ASKING

17

HIDE AND SEEK

What to Do When
You Don't Know What to Do

Since I always read with a pen in my hand, it is not uncommon for me to write questions in the margins of a book. I always appreciate it when I later discover that the writer has anticipated my questions and addressed them. I imagine you have a question or two or ten that you hope will be answered before we reach the end of our time together.

One of those questions is probably, "What should I do when I don't *know* the wise thing to do?" Asking the Best Question Ever will almost always reduce your options, but it won't necessarily single one out. So what then? What should you do if you are genuinely committed to doing the wise thing but you aren't sure which of your options qualifies as the wise choice?

EMOTIONAL STATIC

Wisdom is not always readily apparent. Often the wise choice is obscured by the emotion of the moment. Emotionally charged environments are not conducive to answering the Best Question Ever.

We have all made decisions in the heat of the moment only to regret them later. Excitement over a person, product, or opportunity will skew our perspective. A good salesperson can engage you emotionally in a product. Emotions can make it hard to see straight, think straight, decide straight. This is almost always the case when love, lust, money, or a crisis is involved—these are not emotionally neutral environments.

Most of the decisions we later regret are made when emotions are running high. My guess is that the decision you regret most was made in an emotionally charged moment: Not only were you unable to identify the wise thing to do, but you didn't really care.

But I love him!

Just look at her!

Three hundred horsepower!

Five bedrooms!

A 40 percent return!

No money down!

Negative emotions leave us emotionally out of balance as well. We've all made one or more unwise decisions in the throes of anger, greed, guilt, loneliness, or jealousy. The truth is, when painful emotions are running high, we don't really care about making wise decisions, and so we pretty much do what we feel like doing. We are drawn toward activities that distract us from our pain, and therein lies the problem: It is next to impossible to discern the voice of wisdom when our emotions are raging.

THE KNOW-IT-ALL

An emotionally charged atmosphere isn't the only influence that causes wisdom to elude us. Our ignorance—or shall we say, lack of expertise—can also put wisdom out of reach. There are decision-making environments where our lack of training or education or experience makes it next to impossible to identify valid options, much less sort through them. Unfortunately, our roles as parents, spouses, board members, business owners, etc., often leave us in the precarious position of having to make decisions in specific arenas that lie beyond our core competencies.

As a pastor I run into this all the time. I can't count the times I have sat in, and sometimes led, team meetings where I am expected to shape decisions regarding real estate, construction, sewer easements, rights-of-way, cash sweeps, collars, interest rates, and a plethora of other business-related issues. And each meeting ends somewhat the same way. After all the smart men and women in the room make their case for whatever it is we are trying to decide, they all turn to me and say, "So, Andy, what do you think?"

What do *I* think? I think I need a vacation.

After ten years of looking at financial reports, I'm still not sure whether parentheses on a P&L statement indicate good news or bad. My wife will tell you, I have a difficult time balancing my personal checkbook. And I quit helping our kids with their math homework once they reached the fourth grade. When it comes to numbers, I can pray for wisdom all day, but what I really need is an MBA!

Seminary didn't prepare me to make wise business decisions. Nevertheless, as senior pastor, I am responsible for the business of the church. It is my responsibility to make sure we are following the path of wisdom on the corporate side of things, whether or not it is something I am equipped to do.

REACHING OUR LIMITS

Eventually we all bump up against our limitations. We find ourselves in situations where we are expected to make wise decisions but feel totally inadequate to do so. Parents, remember bringing your first child home from the hospital? Talk about inadequate. How about your first year of marriage? Remember the first time you closed on a house? You signed a hundred documents that you never took the time to read. Why? Because you knew you wouldn't understand them anyway!

So what should you do when you're supposed to know what to do, but don't? What do you do when wisdom is just out of reach but everyone is looking to you, depending on you to know and do the wise thing?

I'll tell you what wise people do: nothing.

Wise people know when they *don't know* and are not so foolish as to pretend they *do* know. Eventually they make a decision and move ahead. But only after they have employed their best-kept secret.

18

KNOWING WHAT YOU DON'T KNOW

The Best-Kept Secret

Get out your pen or marker because I'm about to let you in on the best-kept secret of wise men and women everywhere. This is how they became wise, and it is how they continue to appear wise. This is how they manage to make wise decisions concerning areas of specialty in which they have no expertise. This is how they manage to make wise decisions even in emotionally turbulent decision-making environments. Ready?

Wise people know when they *don't know*, and they're not afraid to go to those who *do know*. When wise people bump up against their limitations, they stop and ask for help.

This is the rule of thumb for wise men and women as it relates to their limitations experientially, academically, and emotionally. They don't deceive themselves; they don't pretend; and they don't act like they're smarter than they really are. They know their limits. They know what they don't know, and they make sure they know someone who does.

This is somewhat counterintuitive. A wise man needing wisdom? That doesn't seem to make any sense. What's the use of being wise if you have to ask for advice? If you need outside input, isn't that evidence of the fact that you really aren't all that wise?

No. Wise men and women frequently seek the counsel of others because that's the wise thing to do. Solomon himself espoused this simple, yet often neglected, principle.

THE WISE GUY

According to the Scriptures, Solomon was the wisest man who ever lived. As a young king, he found himself overwhelmed with the responsibilities that befell him. Then one night the Lord appeared to him in a dream and made him a rather unique offer: "Ask what you wish me to give you" (1 Kings 3:5).

Imagine that! God appearing to a teenager and offering to give him anything he wanted. What would *you* have asked for? Think about it: God offered Solomon a blank check and said, "Fill in the amount." Here's how Solomon responded:

"Now, O LORD my God, You have made Your servant king in place of my father David, yet I am but a little child; I do not know how to go out or come in. Your servant is in the midst of Your people which You have chosen, a great people who are too many to be numbered or counted. So give Your servant an understanding heart to judge Your people to discern between good and evil. For who is able to judge this great people of Yours?" (1 Kings 3:7–9)

I suppose I would have asked for the same thing. Well, maybe not. In fact, "an understanding heart to judge" would have been about the furthest thing from my mind. That probably explains why God didn't make me the same offer when I was sixteen. But Solomon's response was exactly what God was hoping for:

It was pleasing in the sight of the Lord that Solomon had asked this thing. God said to him, "Because you have asked this thing and have not asked for yourself long life, nor have asked riches for yourself, nor have you asked for the life of your enemies, but have asked for yourself discernment to understand justice, behold, I have done according to your words. Behold, I have given you a wise and discerning heart, so that there has been no one like you before you, nor shall one like you arise after you. (1 Kings 3:10–12)

And so Solomon was given wisdom and discernment beyond that of any man or woman who had ever lived. He became the go-to guy for just about everything. He was an architect, poet, philosopher, scientist, scholar, theologian, and ruler—a truly amazing individual.

In the New Testament, you and I are encouraged to follow Solomon's example: "If any of you lacks wisdom, he should ask God, who gives generously to all without finding fault, and it will be given to him" (James 1:5, NIV). This wonderful verse contains an important assumption and a powerful promise. The assumption is that there will be times when we don't know the wise thing to do; the promise is that God will provide us with the wisdom we need. But like Solomon, we must first recognize our need.

That leads us to the Best Question Ever. The wisest man who ever lived insists throughout his writings that, instead of looking within our own hearts for the wisdom we need, we should pursue the counsel of others. In fact, Solomon had more to say about the importance of seeking wise counsel than all the other biblical writers combined.

Here is a random sampling:

A wise man will hear and increase in learning, and a man of understanding will acquire wise counsel. (Proverbs 1:5)

The way of a fool is right in his own eyes, but a wise man is he who listens to counsel. (Proverbs 12:15)

Listen to counsel and accept discipline, that you may be wise the rest of your days. (Proverbs 19:20)

Where there is no guidance, the people fall, but in abundance of counselors there is victory. (Proverbs 11:14)

Without consultation, plans are frustrated, but with many counselors they succeed. (Proverbs 15:22)

You have to stop and ask yourself why the wisest man in the world would put such a premium on seeking advice from others. The answer, of course, is that he was the wisest man in the world! *Wisdom seeks counsel.* The wise man knows his limitations; it is the fool who believes he has none.

My guess is that Solomon remembered how overwhelmed he felt the day he became king, how badly he needed wisdom beyond his years, how discernment seemed hopelessly out of reach. As wise as he became, Solomon never forgot that his wisdom had come from Someone else. And so even after God granted him extraordinary wisdom, Solomon continued to surround himself with trusted advisors.

Don't Leave Home Without It

No one rises above the need for wise counsel. No one. In fact, the more successful we become, the more we need it because there is usually more at stake in the decisions we must make. Violating this simple principle sets otherwise successful people up for failure.

As I write this, three high-profile personalities are battling to stay out of prison. Two of the court cases involve sexual misconduct; the other revolves around mishandled finances. All three have admitted to making "poor choices" or unwise decisions. Regardless of the outcomes of these cases, the reputations of these three people will be tarnished for the rest of their lives. And all three of these expensive, drawn-out court battles could have been avoided if the individuals involved had sought counsel *before* they acted. Even if it turns out that all three are innocent of the charges brought against them, their own unwise decisions set them up for what has followed.

Nobody rises above the need for wise counsel, but many sure do resist seeking it out, which is ironic. After all, the decisions made in private by the aforementioned celebrities eventually became public, and then the public has weighed in on them ever since!

But this dynamic is not limited to those with celebrity status.

19

EVERYBODY'S BUSINESS

You Might as Well Ask

Few people enjoy being told what to do. It's why we couldn't wait to leave home, to strike out on our own, to achieve independence. We resisted our parents' advice, and we've been resisting the advice of others ever since. To complicate things, we are especially resistant to advice in the three areas where we are most vulnerable— the three areas that typically prove to be the sources of our greatest regret: how we allocate our time, spend our money, and handle our relationships.

If you don't believe me, try giving your neighbor advice about how to raise his children. Or walk in uninvited to the office next to yours and explain to a peer how she could make better use of her time. If you're really brave, try explaining to a guy who's buying a lottery ticket that he is throwing away his money.

Let's face it, most of us are hesitant to pursue counsel in the areas where we need it most, and we resist counsel when it is offered. And so in the three areas where we are most vulnerable, we are quick to lean on our own understanding and make decisions that are clouded by our own passion and ignorance.

EVERYBODY'S GOING TO KNOW

But here's an interesting slice of reality to consider: While you may escape having to listen to anyone's opinion about your decisions, you can in no way stop people from forming one. This is the irony of refusing to seek counsel. In many cases, once you have made your decision privately, the outcome will eventually be known publicly. At that point, people will inevitably form an opinion about the wisdom of your choice.

We can convince ourselves that our private lives are nobody else's business. But the results of our personal decisions are rarely private. We often make intensely personal decisions about seemingly private matters, but the effects are felt in the real world and are generally visible to the public.

Everybody knows whom you chose to marry. Your friends know the size, location, and price range of your home. People know what kind of car you drive. Complete strangers know where you work and where you were previously employed. People know whether you went to church last Sunday. And it's no secret whom you choose to spend time with. And whether you like it or not, everybody you know has formed some kind of opinion about all those "private" decisions you have made. It's just human nature.

Before you get too indignant, be honest: You have an opinion about the decisions your friends and relatives have made as well. Don't you?

I can't believe she's dating that guy.

Why are they sending their kids to that school?

Don't they know about the zoning issues in this neighborhood?

He must have dressed in the dark.

There's one other thing to keep in mind about your so-called private decisions: Not only are your decisions known and judged by others, but they also *affect* others. Every decision I make personally and professionally affects other people, every single one. They may seem to be private decisions, but each has public ramifications—repercussions that reach beyond my personal and professional life. As a pastor, every decision I make regarding our church affects a lot of people. The same is true in my role as father and husband.

The same is true for you.

You are not the only person affected by your choices. Chances are, *your* professional and financial security is not the only thing on the line when you make business and money-related decisions, and we've already seen how the consequences of our moral choices can scar others. The news is filled with stories of how thousands of employees have been adversely affected by the foolish decisions of a few greedy executives. All of us know of families that have been splintered because of a decision made by a son or daughter—a decision made in the moment with no thought of how it might impact anyone else. We all know kids who are growing up without a father in the house because Dad made a relationship decision that he thought was nobody else's business.

It may have been none of your business whom your brother or sister chose to marry, but it has impacted your life in some way, hasn't it? As a teenager you convinced yourself that what you did with and to your body was nobody else's business. But you eventually discovered that the consequences of what you chose to do with your body impacted everyone who loved you.

Private decisions have public consequences.

So since your personal decisions will be seen by, judged by, and experienced by others, why not involve others to begin with? Why not benefit from the insight you will be judged by? While it is true that what you choose to do may not be anybody's business, it is equally true that much of what you do will *become* other people's business. They're going to know, they're going to judge, and they might even be significantly affected. So why not invite a few choice people into the decision-making process with you? It certainly won't hurt anything. In fact, it could make all the difference in the world.

20

LISTENING, LEARNING

The Lone Ranger
Wasn't Really Alone

Have you ever stopped and thought about the irony of professional athletes' having coaches? Think about it. Why would a guy who can throw a ninety-five-mile-per-hour fastball over the corner of a rubber plate sixty feet and six inches away need advice on how to pitch from an older fellow who may have trouble *seeing* the plate from that far? Why? Because professional athletes know from experience something wise people seem to grasp intuitively.

Every professional athlete knows that he or she will never reach, nor maintain, peak performance apart from outside input. Granted, the superstar pitcher may be the one with the skill, youth, money, and fame. But none of that is enough to keep him performing at his peak. He needs a coach. He needs another set of eyes and another source of insight to help him judge his performance realistically.

Not coincidentally, men and women who consistently make the right moves relationally, professionally, and financially are those who seek input from others. Again, they know what they don't know and aren't afraid to go to those who do know. And this private habit results in very public success.

INCAPABLE AND INSUFFICIENT

You will never be all you're capable of being unless you tap the wisdom of the wise people around you. Sure, you may get by. You may even do better than most other people. But you will never reach *your full potential* without help and advice from the outside. This is true professionally, spiritually, financially, and even relationally. I say *even* relationally because it can feel so unnatural to seek relational advice, especially at the outset of a relationship.

Think about this. We trust our own feelings going into relationships, whether it be dating, marriage, or business partnerships. Then we cast our lot with lawyers and counselors when leaving those same relationships. Imagine how much pain and chaos would be avoided if people sought wise counsel during the early stages of key relationships instead of putting so much stock in their *feelings*.

Most of us know what it is like to seek counsel on the back end of a relationship that is spinning painfully out of control. Whether it is marriage counseling, pregnancy counseling, or family counseling, it is an attempt to address relational issues that at one time we thought were nobody's business. Again, we have to wonder how much of that could have been avoided if we had sought wise counsel *before* making the decisions that led to the need for wise counsel on the back end.

If you have kids who are old enough to date, you are probably all over this. There's so much you would like to tell them—so many warning signs you would like to point out along the way. You are convinced that if they would just listen to what you have to say, they could avoid a broken heart or worse. But alas, they're a lot like you, aren't they? Not really that interested in what somebody else has to say until things get so painful or complicated that they are forced to listen.

If the Best Question Ever is "What is the wise thing for me to do?" then perhaps the second-best question is, "What do *you* think is the wisest thing for me to do?" As a parent, there are times I would pay big bucks to get my children to ask me that question and mean it. I'm sure my parents would have paid to get me to ask it as well.

WISE AND WISER

One of the realities of being a preacher's kid is that I grew up hearing stories about the complicated situations people had "behaved" themselves into. Looking back, I realize my dad had an agenda in telling me all those stories. I do the same thing with my kids. If it has the same effect on them as it did on me, then so much the better.

The moral of nearly every one of these stories is, "They should have listened." People failed because they didn't listen to God, their parents, their friends, or some other voice of reason. Partly as a result of all those stories, I grew up with a healthy respect for sin. Actually, *fear* may be a better description. But I also grew up knowing that it would serve me well to *listen*.

Why not pause long enough to listen to the people who have faced what we're facing, people who have already been through what we're about to go through and are wiser for their experience? Experience *is* a good teacher, especially if it is other people's experience. There's no point in learning something the hard way if someone else has already paid that price.

I am a better husband because of the wise counsel I received before I said, "I do." Sandra and I are much wiser parents as a result of the incredible insights we learned from the men and women we sought counsel from through the years. I know I am a much better leader because of the advice I have received from the seasoned leaders around me. I don't know if it is fear, insecurity, or wisdom, but I just don't make big decisions without outside input. I don't want to find out what I "should have done" after it is too late to do anything about it.

When we receive wise counsel *after* a decision has been made, it is nothing more than a reminder of how wise we could have been had we asked. But let's face it, sometimes we don't want to ask, do we?

For Him Who Has Ears

Some time ago I was wrestling with what I considered to be a complicated staffing decision. For several nights I talked Sandra's ear off about how complex this situation was and how difficult it was to decide what to do. I reviewed the pros and cons of every option. I expounded on my history with all the personalities involved. I vented my thoughts, my disappointments, and my grievances. But I couldn't decide what would be the wise move.

Sandra listened patiently. But it didn't take long for her to see what was really going on: I knew what I had to do; I just didn't want to do it. So instead, I just kept talking about it. And talking about it. And talking about it. Now, Sandra could have called my bluff, but she is a wise woman who knew it was more important to help her self-deceived husband make the right decision than it was for her to make a point. So instead she asked me, "Why don't you call Steve and see what *he* thinks you should do?"

Steve is one of the wisest men I know, especially when it comes to sorting out personnel issues. Furthermore, I had spent a lot of time with Steve. He had walked me through some truly difficult relational issues. In the process he taught me some invaluable principles that later became reference points for all my relational decisions. I had spent so much time with Steve that often I knew what Steve was going to suggest before he had a chance to suggest it.

Sandra knew that.

When she suggested I call Steve, I blurted out, without thinking, "I *know* what Steve would tell me to do." Sandra just smiled. Mission accomplished.

Face it, one of the primary reasons we don't seek counsel from the wise people around us is that we already know what we are going to hear—and we just don't want to hear it. After all, deceiving ourselves requires a lot of maneuvering, a lot of intentionally dodging the warning signs along the way. The last thing we want is the opinion of an astute individual who will see through our elaborate charade and call us on it!

Several years ago a couple in our church asked me if I would perform the marriage ceremony for their daughter. I don't do many weddings, but I had known this family for quite a while, so I agreed. My last words to them were, "Have Darla call my assistant and we can set up some premarital counseling."

A few weeks later the mother of the bride made an appointment to see me. That was a bit unusual, but I agreed to meet with her. "We love Darla's fiancé," she told me. "We think he's perfect for her. But he's been married before and I want to know what you think about that."

I asked how long ago the man had been divorced. She said he had been separated from his wife for two years. One again I asked, "How long has he been divorced?"

"Three months," she said.

Then I asked a question I knew she didn't want me to

ask. "How long has Darla been seeing Tony?" She hemmed and hawed and finally admitted that they had met a little over a year ago.

As the conversation progressed I realized why she had come. The mother of the bride was interviewing me. Before she subjected her daughter and future son-in-law to my premarital counseling, she wanted to make sure that I wasn't going to say or do anything to throw a kink in their plans.

I informed her that our church had a policy not to remarry anyone until he or she had been divorced at least two years, and that depending upon the circumstances, we might suggest an individual wait even longer.

She shook her head and said, "That's what I had heard."

A few weeks later she called to inform me that they were making other arrangements. I wasn't surprised. But I was mystified. Why would a mother want to shield her daughter and future son-in-law from questions designed to help them think clearly about one of the most important decisions they would ever make? Who would be so foolish as to prioritize a wedding over a marriage? And besides, if Mom was so sure they were perfect for each other, what possible harm could come from their meeting with me? Wouldn't love find a way? Maybe not. Or maybe she wasn't as sure as she pretended to be. Perhaps there was something she didn't want to face. Perhaps there were some realities she and her daughter were working hard to dodge. And dodge them they did. They must be proud.

Mirror Check

The Bible has a term for the person who refuses wise counsel: *fool*. Solomon summed it up this way: "The way of a fool seems right to him, but a wise man listens to advice" (Proverbs 12:15, NIV). In our culture it sounds harsh to refer to someone as a fool, so we soften it by saying, "He acted foolishly" or, "How could I have been so foolish?" But the reality is, when we refuse to listen, when we dodge the truth, when we insist on having our own way, we are fools.

Wise people know when they don't know. The fool is the person who convinces himself that he knows more than he really knows and doesn't need to ask anybody anything. At the end of the day, the wise man breaths a sigh of relief; the fool, a sigh of regret.

Bottom line, when we resist presenting our options to the wise people around us for fear of hearing what we don't want to hear, we are fools. When we insist on ignoring the warning signs and pressing on anyway, we are fools. And in the end, we pay. Fools always pay.

SOS

God knows there will be times when you lack wisdom, times when you will ask the Best Question Ever and come up short.

If you are in the midst of an emotionally challenging situation and circumstances require you to make a decision, go for help.

Don't trust your judgment alone. Just as there are times when physical pain makes us incapable of caring for ourselves, so emotional pain can drive us to the place where we need assistance.

If you are being called upon to make a decision that is out of your league in terms of experience or education, get some help. Don't pretend. Don't fake it. Asking for help is not a reflection of your lack of wisdom. Asking for input is *evidence of* wisdom. When the Best Question Ever doesn't yield the clarity you need, ask somebody you trust, "In light of my past experience, current circumstances, and future hopes and dreams, what do *you* believe is the wise thing for me to do?"

After all, wise people know when they don't know and aren't afraid to go to those who do.

Part VI

THE BEST DECISION EVER

21

PERFECTING YOUR FOLLOW-THROUGH

Painting Inside the Lines

I n light of your past experience, current circumstances, and future hopes and dreams, what is the wise thing for you to do? What do the wise people around you consider the wisest course of action for you to take? These are two extraordinarily powerful questions that you should bring to bear on every area of your life. Acting on the answers to these questions will set you up to live a life of few regrets.

But therein lies the problem: *You have to act.* You have to follow through. For your heavenly Father to leverage the Best Question Ever in your life, you have to act on what you discover. In these final pages I want to help position you for follow-through.

THE GALLERY

Several years ago, toward the end of a long day alone with the kids, Sandra marched everybody to the basement and announced that they were to spend the afternoon painting. She covered a big table with butcher paper, pulled out three small canvases, laid out assorted paints and brushes, and told them that *she* would let *them* know when they were finished!

"Paint what?" asked Andrew, who was nine at the time.

"Anything you please."

"I don't know what to paint," said Allie, who was seven.

"I don't even know *how* to paint," complained Garrett, who was eight.

Without giving further instructions, Sandra headed back upstairs for a well-deserved nap. Thirty minutes later she was awakened by a sound that she rarely heard: silence. No voices. No make-believe explosions. No crying. Nothing. The house was quiet.

Concerned, she headed down the hall to the basement door. No sooner had she opened the door when she heard, "Don't come down yet—we aren't finished." In mama-speak that meant, "Go have a few moments for yourself," an offer Sandra gladly accepted. Twenty short minutes later she heard the pitter-patter of six precious feet scrambling up the basement stairs. "We're ready! We're ready! Come see our artwork!"

What kind of paintings do you suppose were waiting for Sandra at the bottom of the stairs? What kind of art would you expect from three untrained, unattended young children? Three masterpieces? Three introspective self-portraits worthy of hanging in a local gallery?

Why not?

Why is it you imagine unintelligible strokes of paint splattered all over the canvases, the table, and the basement floor? Why are your expectations so low when it comes to my children's artwork?

There's a whole list of reasons. What it all boils down to, however, is that untrained artists won't make the right decisions. Untrained artists don't know the principles and guidelines of painting. They don't know proper technique. Their motives may be pure and their intent noble, but if they don't know how to paint—well, you get the picture.

PLAYING BY THE RULES

There are rules and principles that govern every discipline. Music, architecture, law, education, medicine, athletics, economics, communication, construction, art, finances, accounting—in order to make wise decisions in any of these arenas, you need an understanding of the principles and laws that govern them.

Your accountant cannot give you wise counsel unless he or she knows principles of accounting, along with the tax codes established by the federal government. When you choose a doctor, you assume that person is an expert in his or her field of medicine—you assume this professional knows how the human body works and how to fix it when it quits working. If you hire a builder to build your home, you expect him to understand the applicable government codes and standards as well as the principles of construction.

For the last four years I have been a coach or an assistant coach for my sons' baseball teams. I learned very quickly that knowing the rules and understanding the nuances of Little League baseball make all the difference in a coach's decision-making ability.

For example, in our league there is a five-run limit rule. That is, once a team scores five runs in an inning, their turn at bat is over and the other team automatically comes up to bat. In the sixth and final inning, there are no run limits; however, because of a time limit imposed on Little League games, very few of our games ever make it to the sixth inning.

In spite of the run-limit rule, the coaches in our league typically arrange their batting orders the traditional way— that is, they arrange their lineup so that all their best hitters bat first and all their worst hitters bat at the end of the lineup. But one day it occurred to me that under the circumstances they had it all wrong. If there is a five-run limit each inning, that changes the goal of the game. The goal should be to score five runs *every inning*. So I started arranging our batting order accordingly. Instead of putting our worst batters at the bottom of the order, I sprinkled them throughout the lineup.

Suddenly, we started scoring consistently every inning. And as a result of moving the weaker batters up in the order, something else happened in our favor: The weaker batters started hitting. Moving them up in the order did something for their confidence. We won more games that season than any team in the league.

You see, knowing the way things work makes you a better decision maker. Every decision may not be obvious, but knowing the rules and principles narrows our options and increases our chances of success. If you have ever worked with a professional decorator, you have seen this dynamic at work. There are dozens, maybe hundreds, of ways to beautifully decorate a room. But there are some combinations of fabric and furniture that just won't work, and a good decorator knows which combinations to avoid.

Years ago Sandra and I had a room in our house that we just could not ever make look right. One night when my mom was over, we brought her into our dysfunctional room and said, "Help! What do we need to do?" She moved two pieces of furniture, and it made all the difference in the world. Sandra and I stood there in amazement. "Why hadn't we thought of that?" we wondered.

Simple. My mom is a decorator. She knows the rules.

She took one look at our room and diagnosed the problem. And that brings us to the flip side of this principle.

IT CUTS BOTH WAYS

Generally speaking, when we ignore the rules or principles in any particular field, we pay a price. All the day traders who were active during the dot-com bubble know what I'm talking about. No matter how many times we—um, I mean, *they* were warned to take a long-term approach to securities investing, they just kept on churning their money for short-term gains. And when the bubble burst, a lot of people lost a lot of money. When you ignore the rules, you pay.

This is why people who represent themselves in court usually don't fare very well. They don't know the law. They don't understand courtroom etiquette. They have no experience picking or reading a jury. They don't know the first thing about cross-examining a witness.

I have a friend who decided to improve a piece of land by clearing some trees. He's not a developer. He's not a contractor. (But he has a great personality.) And consequently, he didn't know the proper procedure for improving property inside the city limits. He didn't know you had to have a land disturbance permit. He didn't know that he had specimen trees on his land. He didn't know he was supposed to ask the city arborists to come out and tag trees. He didn't even know there were such things as city arborists. But he does now.

He assumed he could do whatever he wanted to do on his own land. But he was wrong. He didn't know the rules. And after a dozen meetings with the city arborists and a couple of city council members, my friend ended up spending $40,000 to plant trees all over the city as a fine for violating several city ordinances. Next time he will know better. But that was an expensive lesson.

I bet you have a story or two yourself. I bet you wish I would get to my point. Hold on, we are almost there.

HANDS ON

Knowing the rules and principles of a particular discipline is not enough. To harness their power, you must submit to or apply them. When a surgeon performs an operation, he is submitting to the rules and applying the procedures of his particular specialty. No matter how skilled his hands, if he were to ignore proper surgical procedures, the results could be devastating.

Wide receivers can't cut out around the cheerleaders, come back onto the field, and catch a pass without being penalized. Andre Agassi can't serve the ball into the stands and expect to win. The Atlanta Braves can't put ten players on the field at a time. Professional athletes must submit to the rules in order to win.

In every field it is both the knowing and the doing that makes for success. You must first know how things work and then submit yourself to those principles, laws, and techniques. It is what you know and what you do with what you know that make the difference.

So...

22

THE BEGINNING
OF WISDOM

An Act of Surrender

What's true in the realms of medicine, construction, accounting, and sports is true in the core dimensions of your life as well. There are laws and principles that must be adhered to if you are to succeed in the arenas of marriage, parenting, personal finances, friendship, work, and time management. Some of these principles are intuitive; others are not. But knowing and submitting to these principles makes all the difference in the world. For it is within the context of these life rules that wisdom is found. They inform the decision-making process.

Every time you give someone advice, you are drawing upon your insight about how some aspect of the world works. Through the years you have stumbled onto some of these laws and principles. Some you have learned the hard way. You may have been exposed to others through the wisdom of your parents and teachers. But you know a thing or two about how life works. There are certain bad decisions you can spot a mile away. You can see trouble coming. At times you have tried to warn some unsuspecting soul to get out of the way—just like somebody warned you in a previous chapter of your life.

With all of this experience as a backdrop, let me ask you a couple of questions. If I can't expect my children to create a masterpiece on canvas when they do not know and submit to the rules and principles of oil painting, how can we expect to make a masterpiece of our lives without knowing and submitting to the laws and principles of life? If I can't expect my mechanic to make wise decisions about the maintenance of my car without first knowing how the car works, how can I expect to make wise decisions about my family and finances without first knowing the laws and principles that govern these important arenas of life?

Let me take it one excruciating step further. How do you expect to make a masterpiece of your life if you are unwilling to surrender to the Author of life—the One who knows which textures and colors are best blended for the outcome you desire? How do you expect to make wise decisions regarding your family, marriage/love life, and career if you are not willing to submit to the promptings of the One who knows more about those things than you or I ever will?

IN THE BEGINNING

Perhaps it was this line of reasoning that led the wisest man in the world to pen these words: "The fear of the LORD is the beginning of wisdom" (Proverbs 9:10). Wisdom begins with a proper understanding of who God is and who we are not.

Don't rush past this too quickly. Throughout this book I have challenged you to ask *yourself*, "What is the wise thing for me to do?" In the previous section I encouraged you to broaden your audience to a few choice and respected friends. But to fully leverage the Best Question Ever, you need to address it to your heavenly Father. For He is the source of all wisdom, and wisdom begins by properly aligning ourselves with who God is.

Solomon uses the phrase "the fear of the Lord." In this context, "fear" refers to recognition and reverence that leads to submission. You may want to write that down somewhere. Wisdom begins with the *recognition* of who God is. This does not mean simply recognizing His power and knowledge. This is recognizing that you are dealing with the one and only Creator of all things. God with a capital *G*. Wisdom begins when we rightly recognize God's position as God!

Proper recognition results in *reverence*. Reverence is the appropriate response to the One who created and controls all things. The practical side of reverence is submission. Those who recognize and revere the Father have little choice but to embrace His right to rule all that He has created. That moment of recognition and surrender is the beginning of true wisdom.

THE A-HA! FACTOR

Lest we lose sight of the highly relational side of our heavenly Father, Solomon restates his point in different terms. Here's how the entire verse reads:

> The fear of the LORD is the beginning of wisdom, and the knowledge of the Holy One is understanding. (Proverbs 9:10)

Allow me to paraphrase this amazing verse for you this way:

> Wisdom begins when we recognize that God is God and then respond accordingly. The proper response, of course, is surrender. Once we have surrendered, God is more than happy to reveal more and more of Himself. And as we discover more and more of the character and nature of the Father, we gain greater understanding of the world He has created. Our expanded understanding results in an improved ability to choose wisely. Thus, true wisdom begins with a proper recognition of who God is coupled with a proper response—surrender.

If the idea of surrendering to your heavenly Father scares you, consider this: You unknowingly surrender to His principles and laws every day. Every time you make a wise parenting decision, you are applying or surrendering to one of God's principles. Every time you make a wise financial decision, the same thing is true. Every time you submit your body to the knife of a competent surgeon, you surrender yourself to the laws of God. The surgeon is simply making decisions based upon his understanding of the way God created the human body. Every time you submit to a human authority, you are applying one of God's principles.

"But that's different," you argue. "I'm just using good judgment." That may be the way you see it. But if you are simply applying principles that existed before you chose to apply them, you are borrowing from—and recognizing the wisdom of—the Father. Think about it. We have discovered and leveraged principles of physics; we have explored and manipulated the genetic code; we have pinpointed and eradicated many diseases. Our forefathers harnessed high- and low-pressure systems and used them to travel across the seas.

Every single day we benefit from the way God designed things to work. Everything we claim to have created in our human endeavors finds its ultimate source in something God created that we simply discovered and manipulated. Every time we take a breath, we declare our dependency upon and submission to the Father physically. Why then would we hesitate to submit our will? Why are we so afraid to surrender to Him our relationships, our finances, and our careers?

A wise physician does not ignore the way God created the body. A wise accountant does not ignore the principles of mathematics. The beginning of wisdom is recognition of and submission to the One who designed things to work the way things work.

IT'S MUTUAL

One more thought on surrender: It is mutual. Mutual surrender, or submission if you prefer, is one of the most powerful relational dynamics. When two people pledge to put the other first, that is relationship at its best. This is true whether we're talking about a husband and wife, employee and employer, or parent and child. In a relationship of mutual submission, rank and birth order are irrelevant. The point is that each has pledged all that he or she is for the benefit of the other. In a relationship of mutual submission, there is nothing to fear—it is a relationship of trust.

Here's a bit of truth that ought to erase all your misgivings about surrendering to the Father: Before you were born, He submitted Himself to you. On a wooden cross, God sacrificed His best on your behalf. He put you ahead of Himself. Read these words with that thought in mind:

You see, at just the right time, when we were still powerless, Christ died for the ungodly. Very rarely will

THE BEGINNING OF WISDOM 183

anyone die for a righteous man, though for a good man someone might possibly dare to die. But God demonstrates his own love for us in this: While we were still sinners, Christ died for us. (Romans 5:6–8, NIV)

While you had nothing to offer, Christ died for you. He put your sin ahead of His own glory. In this way, He submitted to you. He met your greatest need at great personal expense. To do so, did He demonstrate His authority? No. His right to rule? Nope. Instead, He drew from His vast resources to demonstrate the only thing that would give us the courage to submit fearlessly, courageously: He demonstrated His love. And that demonstration stands as an open invitation for us to respond in kind. And so we are called into a relationship of mutual submission, knowing all the while that our Father took the risk and went first.

I know from my own experience that it is far easier to *believe in* than to *surrender to* God. It's easier to ask myself the Best Question Ever than it is to sincerely ask this question of the Father. But the cross stands as a constant reminder that I have nothing to fear. God can be trusted. After all, He has already demonstrated His unconditional love for me.

THE BEST OF THE BEST

In the end it all comes down to this. Our willingness to ask and respond to the Best Question Ever depends upon our willingness to make the *best decision ever*—the decision to fully submit our lives to our heavenly Father. This is where wisdom begins.

What's true of my children in the realm of art is true of all of us in our lives, relationships, and finances. We know all too well what happens when we paint on our own, when we wave God off in order to choose our own colors, strokes, and textures. Each of us carries the scars, the memories, and the regrets of those seasons when our will took precedence over His.

God desires that your life be a masterpiece that reflects His greatness and your uniqueness. But to create a masterpiece with our lives, we must submit ourselves to the hand of the Master. We must allow Him to influence each stroke on the canvas of our lives.

So let me ask you, Have you made the best decision ever? Have you fully surrendered all of you to all of Him? Have you predecided to submit to His will before you know what He will ask? If not, I can't think of a more appropriate way to end our time together than to give you an opportunity to pray a prayer of surrender. There's nothing special about these words. It is the attitude of your heart that will make the difference.

Heavenly Father, today I place myself under
Your authority. I surrender all of me to You.
As You demonstrated Your love for me

through the death of Your Son, so I desire to demonstrate my love for You through a renewed mind and surrendered will. Thy will be done in me. I surrender all. In the name of my Savior, I pray. Amen.

EPILOGUE

It is possible to live life with few regrets. Regret-free living is found on the path of wisdom. So as we part ways let me ask you one more time.

What is the wise thing for you to do?

In light of your past experience, your current circumstances, and your future hopes and dreams, what is the wise thing for you to do?

A wise man put it this way:

> He who trusts in his own heart is a fool, but he who walks wisely will be delivered. (Proverbs 28:26)

My hope for you is that you would walk wisely and experience God's deliverance all the days of your life.

"Andy Stanley offers a fresh perspective on ageless truths that will be of enormous benefit to today's leaders and to future generations."
— Patrick S. Flood, chairman and CEO, HomeBanc Mortgage Corporation

DON'T MISS THESE TITLES FROM ANDY STANLEY

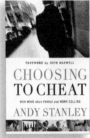

CHOOSING TO CHEAT
Choosing to Cheat presents a strategic plan for resolving the tension between work and home—reversing the destructive pattern of giving to your company and career what belongs to your family.

ISBN 1-59052-329-6

HOW GOOD IS GOOD ENOUGH?
Find out why Jesus taught that goodness is not even a requirement to enter heaven—and why Christianity is beyond fair.

ISBN 1-59052-274-5

THE NEXT GENERATION LEADER
Be the kind of leader you'd admire! Find inspiration, encouragement, and proven advice from pastor and bestselling author Andy Stanley.

ISBN 1-59052-046-7

VISIONEERING
Andy Stanley shows readers how to set goals and obliterate the obstacles to a passionately lived, meaningful life. He offers a workable plan for discovering a life vision aligned with God's own vision.

ISBN 1-57673-787-X

Available at Christian bookstores everywhere
www.multnomahbooks.com

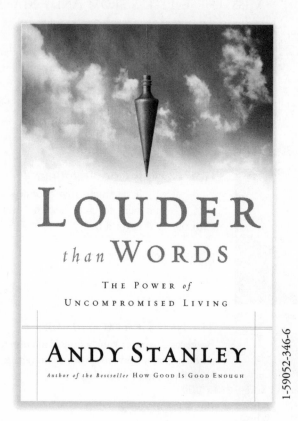

LOUDER
than WORDS

THE POWER *of*
UNCOMPROMISED LIVING

ANDY STANLEY

Author of the Bestseller HOW GOOD IS GOOD ENOUGH

1-59052-346-6

Sharing a strategy for personal character development, Andy Stanley helps you determine your personal definition of success and introduces a step-by-step program for prioritizing your life, overcoming barriers, and more.

Multnomah

www.multnomahbooks.com

DON'T MISS THESE ADDITIONAL MINISTRY TOOLS FROM ANDY STANLEY AND NORTHPOINT RESOURCES!

7 PRACTICES OF EFFECTIVE MINISTRY

Bestselling author Andy Stanley is joined by two respected ministry specialists to give pastors an insightful and entertaining parable for every church leader who yearns for a more simplified approach to ministry.

ISBN: 1-59052-373-3

DISCOVERING GOD'S WILL
STUDY GUIDE

Designed for small groups or personal study, this companion study guide to the *Discovering God's Will* DVD will take readers through the important steps of decision making.

ISBN: 1-59052-379-2

PARENTAL GUIDANCE REQUIRED
STUDY GUIDE

This six-session companion study guide to the *Parental Guidance Required* DVD is a practical resource that will encourage parents to closely examine the relationships in their children's lives.

ISBN: 1-59052-381-4

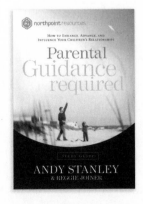